**YO**

# YOUR DOGS TRAINING

CHARLIE WYANT
and
PETER LEWIS

*Illustrations by Peter Davies*

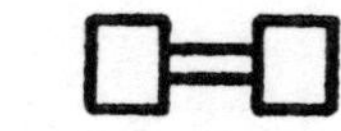

**Canine Publications**

**CANINE PUBLICATIONS**
50 George Street, Portsmouth
Hampshire. Tel: Portsmouth 754808

ISBN 0 906422 02 7 (Case bound)
ISBN 0 906422 03 5 (Paper back)

First Published 1979



Printed in Great Britain by Brown & Son (Ringwood) Ltd., Crowe Arch Lane,
Ringwood, Hampshire.

# CONTENTS

# ILLUSTRATIONS

**ILLUSTRATIONS** *(cont.)*

## ABOUT THE BOOK

The decision to become a dog owner should never be taken lightly for a dog needs constant attention exercise feeding and above all, training All this adds up to time and expense, but the joy of owning a faithful, well trained four legged friend, has little comparison Always pleased to see you and to do your bidding, their company is rarely a nuisance to anyone and is a source of pride and pleasure to the owner

We have had dogs around us for many years and find it unthinkable to be without them. This has led us both to spend a great part of our lives in the pursuit of better understanding of the dog and the most logical and kindest methods of training A dog so submissive that he is afraid of his owner is not a pleasant sight, neither would have been the training methods used An untrained dog is a nuisance to everyone, so there has to be a happy medium of mutual love and respect which can only be brought about by careful teaching.

Having felt for some years that there was a need for an inexpensive concise book dealing solely with household training and care, we have put our heads together to produce this book. We make no apologies for the chapter on the responsibilities of the owner for it is something that has to be said particularly in this day and age

We hope that you will come to understand the

dog and therefore be in a better position to educate him to be a model member of the canine world. Having done so, join a local dog training club whose instructors will be able to give you invaluable personal attention and advice, then we feel sure that it is unlikely that your dog will be considered anti-social.

Charlie Wyant & Peter Lewis.

# Chapter 1

## THE RESPONSIBILITIES OF DOG OWNERSHIP

In recent years those of us involved in the dog world have witnessed with alarm the growth of the anti-dog lobby in this country. Newspapers, television and radio are very quick to latch on to "a good news story" that portrays adverse comments on something that a dog, its owner or both, have done or failed to do. We all know that the media favour bad news in all walks of life and rarely quote instances of life that are normal. Some local authorities are now being swayed by the anti-dog publicity, placing restrictions on dogs in parks and other amenity areas. At the moment authorities with such views are in the minority, but irresponsible dog ownership only adds fuel to the fire.

To be totally condemmed are the owners who allow their dogs to roam the streets or public places unattended, such people are not dog lovers and do those of us who love our canines a great dis-service. Unfortunately those same people are unlikely to read a book such as this, having little interest in the training of their dog or its general welfare.

### Your Dog and the Neighbours

A trained, well cared for dog, will not be a nuisance to other people. One cannot keep a dog without realising that the next door neighbour may not be a dog lover. You are likely to become enemies if the dog jumps the fence and wanders all over your neighbours garden, digs holes in his flower beds or continually barks at his cat. No matter how wonderful your pet may be to you, he will not appear wonderful to the neighbour.

## Fouling on Beaches and Streets

We are also faced with owners who would be horrified if they were accused of not being dog lovers, yet whose actions or lack of them, are almost as irresponsible. Have you ever sat on a beach on a sunny day and had an unruly dog running around kicking sand in your face as he charges by? Have you ever stepped in dogs excreta? If so you will know how offensive and unpleasant it is. Have you ever been nipped or bitten by a dog, who with such a tendency, should be kept completely under control? Let's face it not everyone likes animals of any description let alone dogs, and we should not inflict our dogs good or bad habits upon others. If we do then we create greater arguments for more restrictions to be placed upon a dogs freedom.

On the beach dogs should be kept on a lead and only exercised below the high water line. In the street a dog should always be under the controlling influence of the lead no matter how well the owner has trained him. The finest trained dog in the country can never be 100% reliable, for anything is liable to cause him to panic and run out into the road causing a traffic accident, perhaps with fatal consequences. Now and again we have been asked by dog owners how to stop their dogs chasing cars or bicycles. Whilst a cure can be effected by causing an unpleasant association with such vehicles, that is not the real answer. Yes, you've guessed. The dog should never be in a situation where he can chase cars. Where there is traffic nearby the dog should be on a lead. Of all the dogs we have owned the case of a car-chasing dog has never arisen because they have not been given the opportunity. Likewise, even with a dog on the lead, he should never be allowed to foul pavements or foot-paths. If he looks like doing so he should be taken to the gutter before the act commences. Even a well trained dog can have an accident, so to cover this possibility the owner can keep a small polythene bag in his pocket. If the hand is placed inside the bag the mess can easily be picked up, then using the other hand the bag can be turned inside out so that there is no need to touch the contents and it can be taken home to be disposed of.

## Dogs and Shops

There are rightly many restrictions about taking dogs into shops, particularly those which sell food, so in the absense of someone to wait outside with the dog, he is best left either in the car or at home. Exteriors of shops seldom have any posts or brackets to which a dog can be tied, but if this can be done the owner must ensure that the dog is of suitable temperament to be tied on a busy pavement. Jumping up to make friends with passers-by will not be welcome, but far worse is the dog that guards his immediate surrounds when restricted by the lead for this may lead to biting. If confident that the dog will not be a nuisance, play safe by only leaving him tied for a few minutes just allowing sufficient lead to enable him to sit or lie down.

## Car Ventilation

If during hot weather the dog is left in a car it is the owners responsibility to ensure that it is adequately ventilated. All windows should be opened but only sufficiently to ensure that he cannot escape or put his head through the gap to exercise a guarding instinct. Remember that if the dog is left in the car for a long period, what might have originally been a shady place can finish up exposed to the sun. If the dog does not have sufficient air he can be caused much distress, with his death possibly being the final result.

## Identity Discs and Dog Licences

A dog should wear an identity disc stating the owners name, address and telephone number, for even responsible dog owners can lose a dog through no fault of their own. Maybe you have noticed that I have made no mention of the dogs name being shown on the disc, for this information only makes it easier for dog thieves to carry out their evil occupation. Yes, it does happen. Unscrupulous people steal dogs for a variety of reasons, the worst being where they are subsequently sold for gain to be used for vivisection purposes.

Once a dog is six months of age the law demands that a dog licence is obtained, and this can be purchased at any post office. Whilst the fee has for many years been very cheap, it is quite possible that it will be increased at some time in the future. Arguments have raged in the dog world for several years over this very question. There are pros and cons, but it remains to be seen what will happen.

## Third Party Insurance

The owner of a dog should ensure that he is covered for third party insurance for any damage that his dog causes as he can be found liable in court for compensation. A dog can damage farm animals, destroy a fence and many other things, which is not only anti-social but will be an unwanted expense. Far worse is a dog that causes damage to humans either directly or by being the cause of a road accident with possible loss of life. Some insurance companies offer this type of cover as part of the normal household insurance, and there are also one or two who specialise in canine insurance. Many dog training clubs have an arrangement with these specialist companies whereby the annual subscription to the club includes insurance or a small figure is added to the subscription as a surcharge. If you belong to a dog club and are unsure whether the subscription includes insurance, be safe and ask one of the club officials. Alternatively ask an insurance agent or contact one of the specialist companies. Insurance is usually something we don't want until we are in trouble, but wise is the dog owner who ensures he is covered.

## Rabies

The threat of rabies has been taken very seriously indeed, and in fact the government have conducted a massive publicity campaign in recent years. This is to their credit, for almost without exception the dog world is behind them. We are an island country and have always kept rabies out successfully. However, with modern living and the growth of travel for everyone, the threat becomes greater. Quarantine regulations might appear to be a nuisance to some, but they are there to protect not only the humans of this country but the animals as well. An outbreak of rabies would mean compulsory muzzling of dogs, and in some cases instant destruction. For a dog lover that is bad enough, but more important is that it is a killer and humans having contracted this disease can die in a most painful manner. A bad outbreak of rabies would also add much fuel to the fire of the anti-dog lobby As a responsible dog owner never attempt to break the quarantine laws, and inform the authorities by dialing 999 immediately should you think these laws are being infringed As dog lovers we have a duty to protect both the populace and our dogs from this dreaded disease

## Caring for the Dog

So far we have dealt with the possible effects of dogs on other people, but we have a responsibility to the dog who is going to be so dependant upon us He will need a lot of attention and education, so it is wise to know what is in store should the decision be made to keep a dog Just as one has a bedroom, the dog needs a place of his own with a comfortable, dry warm bed, toys of his own and the right equipment for his walks.

The new dog owner will probably start off with good intentions to walk the dog at least once a day but self discipline may have to be exerted during the middle of winter when it is cold, wet and muddy It will be a bore to leave the warmth of the house missing what promised to be a good television programme, but it has to be done Grooming is another necessity that can become a chore, but every dog needs to be brushed regularly as a matter of cleanliness, which will also avoid his coat becoming matted and tangled.

How often is basic domestic training overlooked? Unfortunately, all too often Without any knowledge of how to bring up a well controlled dog, some owners hope that he will improve of his own accord This is rarely the case and whilst this book offers some advice on a dogs general welfare, it is primarily aimed at helping dog owners to teach their dogs acceptable behaviour. It has often been said that "a trained dog is a happy dog" and this statement is very true. A dog is an animal that cannot reason and therefore the owner is unable to explain to him the rules of living. Consequently the untrained dog is constantly confused as to why his owner is sometimes pleased or displeased with his actions or lack of them. A trained dog, which normally means a trained owner as well, is in a much better position of understanding. He is therefore less confused and much happier. It should be realised that as a dog can live in excess of fifteen years, he should never be purchased in the first place if his welfare and interests are going to be a five minute wonder.

## Dog Training Clubs

There are many dog training clubs throughout the country, who for many years have offered an inexpensive community service by teaching people how to train their own dogs. A list of such clubs is to be found at the end of this book, showing the name of the person to contact, the area in which the classes are held and the training night. Much can be learned from a book such as this, but for what amounts to a very small fee these clubs offer exceptional value for money. Apart from receiving instruction on general training or advice on specific training problems, the very fact that a dog has to socialise with his fellow canines plus people from outside of his immediate home environment, is of great advantage. Usually if a dog appears over-aggressive to his species or snaps at people passing by, it is because he has not been socialised when young. Over-friendly dogs can be just as much of a nuisance as the timid ones that hang back in fear. For instance whilst walking such a dog towards people he may jump up to lick a face or leap on a childs shoulders, thereby knocking them over which will make his friendly approach far from welcome. Timid dogs are the ones who are inclined to nip or bite, which presents the owner with a difficult problem. Not only is there a total lack of knowledge of how to cure the ill, but it is unlikely that suitable facilities are available at home. A dog training club will have knowledgeable instructors, with people and dogs being the facilities. Even dogs of perfect temperament benefit from such socialisation.

Many clubs will not accept a puppy until he is six months of age although some do accept younger dogs. The classes are often very popular necessitating the operation of a waiting list, so it is advisable to contact the secretary of the chosen club as soon as a dog or puppy has been acquired.

## Chapter 2

# BUYING A DOG

### Choosing a Suitable Breed

Having made the decision to become a dog owner with all the attendant responsibilities to the dog and other people, we must now consider how the suitability of the environment in which we live should have some influence on our choice. If living in a reasonably large house in the country with access to open spaces, then virtually any size of dog would be suitable. However the countryside is often comprised of roads and lanes that separate farmland, making it difficult to find suitable places to let the dog run free. It can be, that with facilities such as parks or recreation grounds, the town dweller has better opportunities for exercise, so all local amenities must be taken into consideration. Residents of small high rise flats in built up areas would be unwise to choose a large breed, it being cruel to keep breeds such as Irish Wolfhounds, Alsatians or Labradors under such circumstances. Whilst it is not altogether wise to keep any dog in a flat, some of the very small breeds are content in such conditions providing they are regularly taken out for exercise.

Although it goes without saying that a large dog requires far more exercise than a small one it is amazing how many dog owners ignore this requirement, for much of the obesity seen in dogs is due to lack of exercise rather than overfeeding. The sporting breeds such as retrievers require much exercise, so if you do not have the facilities, or if honest do not think that you will continue to exercise the dog properly throughout his life, choose a smaller breed. It is a fact that the smaller breeds tend to get under the feet, whilst with the larger ones this happens less often. The small breeds are often fidgets whilst larger dogs are more easily seen or will often find a corner of the room out of the way. It is wrong to assume that large dogs make more noise than those that are smaller but what is usually true is that the former, whilst having a bark of greater volume do so less frequently at a less irritating pitch.

The Border Collie may look very appealing showing much intelligence when working sheep, but it should be remembered that years of selective breeding have brought about this instinct for work which he will need to be given. Some breeds that have an appearance or reputation for being fierce very often have a soft nature. These days people seem to require more than a pet, feeling that a larger dog will give more security from rogues or house intruders, although small dogs whether pedigree or mongrel are ideal for barking at strangers. The great respect all people have for Alsatians or Dobermanns may well be a deterrent, but remember that it is unfair to put a large dog in a small place without sufficient exercise.

The prospective owner must also consider the cost of feeding a dog, taking into account that one of Alsatian size will require approximately two pounds of food a day whereas breeds such as terriers require considerably less, ten to twelve ounces a day probably being sufficient.

## The Choice of a Dog or Bitch

It is wise to understand the implications of

keeping either a dog or a bitch. A healthy dog will always show interest in the opposite sex of the species but sometimes his sexual urge will get him into trouble. Although some dogs can have a greater interest in this direction than others it is an instinct that nature intended. A dog being exercised whilst restricted by the lead will remember where he came across the scent of a bitch in season, later attempting to escape the confines of the house to track her down. Also if untrained he can constantly be pulling towards other dogs in the street in the hope of finding a female who may be in season.

The owner of the bitch has to contend with her having a strong mutual attraction to the male dog during her season. This will first occur at between eight or nine months of age with a recurrence at between six and twelve month intervals. There are pills and aerosol products on the market which help to counteract the scent which is so attractive to the male of the species. The aerosols can be sprayed on the bitch and the entrances to where she lives, although the use of them is no guarantee that the local romeo will be fooled.

Whilst it is difficult to generalise, other than during her season a bitch can be the more faithful companion than the dog for she has less distractions. A dog and a bitch left together rarely fight seriously, but when two bitches start fighting, even mother and daughter, they can fight to the death if left unattended. If two bitches show aggressive tendencies towards each other they will need to be kennelled in such a way that will make it impossible for them to fight, or alternatively harden the heart and find a good home for one of them. When considering the acquisition of a second bitch bear this possible problem in mind.

Two dogs are more likely to fight than two

bitches, or a dog and a bitch, but in the latter circumstances spare a thought for the frustrations of the dog during his female friends season period.

When buying a second dog it is wise that it should be a puppy, for the older animal will have a certain amount of inherent mothering instinct towards the youngster carefully keeping him in his place. If another strange adult dog is introduced into the household fighting is more likely to occur, for the original dog may well object to the newcomer on what he considers to be his own patch.

## Where to Buy a Puppy

There are many sources from which you can purchase a dog, such as advertisements in the local paper by pet stores or owners of bitches that have produced a litter. It is quite possible to make a wise purchase from any of these sources but generally speaking the safest way is to approach the professional breeder who should be an expert. If unable to locate a suitable litter of your chosen breed there are various magazines that contain a wealth of information. The Kennel Gazette is obtainable from the Kennel Club, or alternatively weekly magazines available from newsagents such as Our Dogs and Dog World.

A crossbreed or mongrel can make an ideal pet becoming a faithful companion for life, but there are advantages and disadvantages to such an acquisition. Often being the result of an unplanned mating a crossbreed costs less money to purchase than the pedigree dog. Such a mating can lessen the chance of hereditary defects. A great disadvantage is that although the litter of puppies may look very similar as babies they can all grow up to be entirely different shapes and sizes. The known ancestry of the pedigree dog, whilst not guaranteeing a perfect dog in every respect, does give an idea of likely temperament, looks and size, and whether the lines from which he has been bred have a tendency to any of the hereditary defects. You might have the opportunity to acquire an adult dog, be it from friends, an advertisement or from a body such as the R.S.P.C.A. Again it is possible to make a wise selection, but you are unlikely to know much about the background of the particular dog or any vices he may have previously acquired. One must also consider that it is easier to settle a puppy than an adult dog into a household.

## Hereditary Defects

There are a number of hereditary defects affecting every breed, and as the name implies they are passed on through the generations. In recent years they have become more of a problem with the pedigree dog. One whole chapter could be devoted to this subject, but in a book such as this it is better to name some of the more prevalent defects together with the possible consequences. For a household dog the most dangerous to the human is Epilepsy, particularly where there are children, for a dog having a fit does not know what he is doing so his jaws are likely to seize upon anything in his way. With this complaint the fit can be over in a matter of minutes with the dog appearing perfectly normal again. Should you discover your dog having a fit keep well away from him until it has passed and seek veterinary advice as soon as possible. Epileptic fits do not usually occur when the dog is occupied in some manner, it being more likely that whilst the dog is quiet the brain becomes over active with a resultant fit. The disease can sometimes be controlled by medication but control cannot be guaranteed, therefore if veterinary experts feel that the Epilepsy is worth trying to control it is far safer to keep the dog kennelled.

Another defect that can have the effect of the dog seeming to have a poor temperament when in fact he is suffering from blindness, is Progressive Retinal Atrophy. This can manifest itself at the age of three months with total blindness being the result at a year to three years in the worse cases. A dog naturally uses his nose as much as his eyes to find out what is going on around him, so dependent upon the degree of blindness he will use his nose to an even greater extent, therefore disguising from his owner the fact that he is blind. This progressive defect of the retina of the eye known as PRA can cause a dog to growl or lift his lip at anyone because something has suddenly come into his blurred vision putting him on guard. The same thing can happen to a dog that is deaf, for in this instance he is suddenly confronted with what might appear to be danger before his ears have been able to warn him of the approach.

Whilst there are many other defects the remaining major one is Hip Dysplasia. The incidence of HD affects most breeds and mongrels with the notable exception of Greyhounds. A bad case of this disease can have the effect of giving the dog little control of the back half of the body even to the extent of him being unable to rise or walk.

## Children, Babies and Dogs

Even an aggressive dog will display gentleness with a puppy and so will an adult dog with young children of the family, it being very rare to find problems in this direction. However, children who grow up with their own family dog must be cautioned against expecting other dogs that they meet to display the same characteristics. It is very wrong to put into a childs mind a fear of other dogs, but never allow a child to rush up to a strange dog for the intention can be misinterpreted. Far better that a strange dog is approached slowly so that he has time to assess the situation. Dogs brought up with children usually finish up as better members of the communtiy in as much as they are subjected to far more household hustle and bustle. Whilst most people love a puppy, a child will spend more frequent periods playing with him than the average adult, forging a mutual lifelong friendship.

A dog can live in a childless household where he is the centre of attention. If a baby is born into that household problems can arise, for we all know that a new baby is immediately the centre of attention, dog or no dog. The petting and fuss that all the family make towards the new arrival means that the dog, whilst not completely ignored, is no longer the sole apple of everyones eyes. Just as an older child can become jealous of the new baby, so can a dog. The introduction of the dog to the baby must be carried out quite carefully, invariably with the dog tied up whilst he is patted and fussed at the same time as the baby is being spoken to. Once a dog has accepted a child they become absolute companions which makes good company for both child and dog.

### Kennel Club Registration

A pedigree dog, once registered with the Kennel Club and with the ownership transferred to your name, can take part in any event held under Kennel Club rules and regulations. It may be that when purchasing a dog there is no thought of breeding from him or competing in recognised competitions.

However, people do change their minds, so it is prudent to ensure when he is obtained that the dogs official paperwork is initiated. Only the breeder can initiate the registration, so when negotiating the deal check with him that the dog is being registered. The breeder should also be able to supply the transfer or ownership form which must contain the breeders signature, and once completed should be forwarded to the Kennel Club with the appropriate fee.

Whilst mongrels and crossbreeds obviously cannot be registered to allow them to compete in breed classes at dog shows, they are not entirely excluded from competition for they can be entered in the Obedience and Working Trials Register which will enable them to compete in such events. Applications for this or any form should be made to The Kennel Club, 1 Clarges Street, Piccadilly, London W1Y 8AB who will also advise on the current requirements to register dogs.

# Chapter 3

# YOUR DOG AT HOME

## To Kennel or not

Whether or not to keep the dog in an outside kennel is an important decision best taken long before he is brought home. Whilst it is somewhat unfair to transfer an adult dog to a kennel once he has become accustomed to the comforts and companionship of a house, if as a young puppy he is housed in a kennel he will readily adapt to his environment. It must be remembered that man has domesticated what was originally a wild animal, so his coat is quite adequate to protect him from the cold of the winter night providing that he has dry reasonably draughtproof quarters. Professional dog breeders rear their litters in kennels by necessity, so therefore a puppy taken home to a kennel is only going to a change of location. The fact that he may spend the first few nights crying is not because he is in a kennel but because he misses the companionship of his brothers and sisters, with the added confusion of the strange surroundings. Litters reared in the house by the breeder can go straight into a kennel but it may take a little longer for them to adapt.

If the decision is made to kennel, the old idea of a small two by three foot wooden box with a sloping roof plus a hole at the front is really not sufficient. Far more suitable is a garage, garden shed or any converted outbuilding which should have a secure outdoor run attached to it. Dependent upon the size of the dog to be housed, the kennel should be a bed with a wooden floor raised between three and ten inches from the ground with sides all round of up to a foot high. This bed should be of a size that will allow the full grown dog to lie stretched out. Blankets, rugs or other suitable materials can be placed on this raised platform which the dog will soon snuggle into. Should the floor of the building be wooden then a coat of varnish will make it more impervious to moisture if accidents happen. For the same reason when the dog is housed indoors, whilst he needs a place which he recognises to be his own, it is better that the room he sleeps in has a floor that can easily be cleaned.

Dogs can be trained to only enter certain rooms or to stay in one room if that is the wish of the owner. However, with all training , consistency is the key. If he is allowed across the threshold today it cannot be expected of him to realise that tomorrow he may not enter. Right from the very first day he enters the house his boundaries must be determined, whilst a careful watch is kept to ensure that should any attempt be made to cross the demarcation line, he is scolded and put back. With a very young puppy it would be better to keep doors shut until he knows the meaning of the word 'no', thus avoiding confusion.

The majority of dog owners would find life much more pleasant if their dogs were trained to spend some time in a kennel. For example when guests arrive the dog can become a nuisance, especially an exhuberant puppy of six months. With low modern furniture the coffee cups are soon swept to the floor with the result that the dog is in trouble without really understanding why. If he will happily stop in a kennel and run with his own toys, the house can safely be left without returning to find the carpet, furniture or other articles ruined. Such things happen because of boredom, also if left for any lengthy duration the dog will by necessity have needed to relieve himself. Upon return it is all very well and good to scold him for something he did hours ago, but it will not have the effect of catching him in the act. Far better that the dog is accustomed to occasionally being left in a kennel out of harms way.

A noisy kennelled dog can be very irritating to neighbours, so try to stop it by shouting 'Quiet', taking action at the same time. If a sheet of tin or corrugated iron is put by the kennel or forms an integral part of the run, it can be put to good use by throwing a stone against it. The sudden noise plus a command will usually bring immediate peace.

## A Puppy's First Night

It is preferable to bring the puppy home well before darkness or the household bedtime allowing him to gain a certain amount of confidence in his new surroundings before being confined to a room or kennel for the night. Avoid feeding him until he has been at home for some hours so that he is really hungry, consuming all the food put before him. A good breeder will have provided a diet sheet so that at least for the first few critical days of settling in, his food is the same, thus avoiding some unnecessary change of life style. Even better is the breeder who will let you have sufficient food to cover those first few days so that should you wish to change his diet, it can be done gradually.

If buying a six to eight week old puppy it is advisable to ignore any noise that he will undoubtedly make during the first night or two. When crying or barking, the more you go back to the puppy to fuss it the longer will sleepless nights continue. Far better to have it all over and done with once two or three nights have passed rather than feeling so sorry for him that eventually he will be in your bed. If, prior to the household bedtime the puppy is left to sleep for two or three hours, trouble can be expected when he awakens just as everyone has gone to bed. For the first night the best approach is to allow the puppy to become quite tired and hungry so that after feeding sleep is the necessary result. A stone hot water bottle wrapped in a blanket will help simulate the warmth of his lost family, and one or two toys left in his bed may amuse him when he awakens.

## Feeding the Puppy

A six to eight week old puppy will require four meals a day which can gradually be reduced to one main meal at 8 to 10 months of age. Two of the four meals should be milky based, with baby foods such as Farex being ideal whilst the puppy is very young. This can be mixed with cows milk or any of the several canine powdered milks containing vitamin additives that are available these days. Some roughage in his diet is essential, particularly as he gets older. Biscuits soaked in milk or with water added are suitable, alternatively they can be fed dry. For the dogs meaty meal Woffle is a very safe food which is excellent for young dogs as it doesn't upset their tummies, particularly if they have been reared on it. Mince from the butcher can be used, but in either case biscuit meal should be added.

The timing of the four meals is best spread over the hours the family is not in bed. For instance the puppy can have a meat based breakfast followed by milky lunchtime and teatime feeds, with the remaining meaty meal being given last thing at night. Some additives can be mixed with the dogs meals of which there are several multi-vitamin canine products available. Such products usually contain a good balance of vitamins which help to ensure that the puppy will grow to be strong and healthy.

### Feeding the Adult dog

Once the dog is an adult he will need to be fed once a day. This can be done at any time, but whatever the chosen part of the day it is preferable to feed within a two hour period. A dog always fed at exactly a certain time can make a lot of fuss if household circumstances require a change.

There are many dog food products available today. Tinned dog food is something we all aware of, which is usually meat based containing varying amounts of meat according to the quality and price. It is normal to add a biscuit meal which will provide the roughage, but there are other products which the manufacturers claim to be a complete diet. Many people feed their dogs with either raw or cooked tripe which is not always easy to obtain or the most pleasant smelling food to handle, but mixed with some biscuit meal it makes a nourishing feed. Scraps from the household plates are another way to feed but usually a sufficient amount cannot be guaranteed. Pork is generally regarded as being unsuitable, and never give the dog chicken for fear that the small bones will stick in his throat. Whilst mutton bones will splinter a marrow bone will not. giving most dogs hours of enjoyment. Apart from the vitamins they contain, the constant chewing will help to keep the teeth free from scale and the gums in good order. Dogs love to chew something, so far better that they should chew a bone rather than the leg of a chair.

A most important point to ensure is that the food dish can be put in front of the dog to be subsequently taken away again whilst he is still eating. This also applies to bones or to his toys, for a dog that will not allow you to do so is going to be a hazard. If walking too near these things he may well bite to remind you to keep away, and if there are any young children in the house this behaviour could be very dangerous. A dog that has such manners has developed a guarding instinct of what he considers is his own property, which must be stopped very quickly by scolding or, if necessary, by giving him a shaking as well. With a puppy, food should be removed and then replaced whilst he is eating, with corrective measures being taken where necessary.

## House Training

This is always a problem to new dog owners but it really is quite simple. The most important point to understand is that a puppy will always want to relieve himself shortly after sleep, food or drink. The owner must be on guard at these vulnerable times, taking the puppy outside to the place it is preferred that he should carry out these bodily functions. As soon as he does so he must be praised and given a command such as 'Be quick', 'Duties', or whatever is the chosen word or phrase. The command will mean nothing to him at first, but over a long period he will associate it with relieving himself so that when adult it will be possible to indicate to him what he is required to do.

With a puppy in the house accidents will happen. When they do, clean them up with some old newspaper and place the soiled newspaper in the part of the garden that you wish the puppy to use. Next time be more vigilant by taking him regularly to this area, particularly at the vulnerable times. Usually the smell of the soiled paper will create in the young puppy's mind an association of ideas so that he believes he has relieved himself in that place before. Hitting the dog with rolled newpaper is not the way to set about curing the problem, it being purely a question of vigilance plus commonsense.

Should disinfectant be used where the puppy has had an accident, take care that it is not too strong. Over-strong solutions can damage his paws or get into his stomach. Sitting in a wet patch of such solution may affect his private parts so some thought and care is needed when final cleaning of accidents includes the use of disinfectants.

## Worming

Roundworms are the most common to be found in the young dog. All puppies are likely to be affected with them no matter how careful the breeder has been. A good breeder will have wormed the litter at least twice before the puppies are taken away, but because evidence of worms cannot be seen in the dogs motions it must not be assumed that he is worm free. The cycle of the worm is such that should there be any in the intestine the eggs will be in the bloodstream. Whilst worm tablets will kill off the ones in the intestine, the eggs will find their way back to this part of the body via the bloodstream, thus two dosages are necessary. The best method is to ask your veterinary surgeon for suitable medication, or alternatively purchase one of the products manufactured by Sherleys which are stocked by Boots or good pet shops. The instructions should be carefully followed, which will include the dosage for age, size and weight of the dog and should not be exceeded. Puppies should be treated for roundworm several times up to the age of six months, but an adult dog need not be wormed unless trouble is suspected.

Tapeworms are not as likely to infect a dog as roundworms. If they do the dog will usually have reached nine to ten months before they become apparent. One needs to keep a wary eye on the dogs motions for tapeworm. Whilst it can be several feet in length, it will break off in small white segments rather like grains of rice, which will be passed by the dog. There are products available for this problem or a vet will prescribe the necessary medication.

Another type of worm is the hookworm which is not visible. They bury through the dogs stomach and suck the blood. The signs are that the dog will be out of sorts, appearing listless. His coat will most likely be harsh with his motions usually black and soft while the eyes when inspected will have a yellowish pinky hue instead of being a nice bright colour. Should you suspect this type of worm has infected the dog, take a sample of his motions to the vet who will analyse it and if necessary prescribe the appropriate medication.

### Inoculations

At about eight to ten weeks of age a puppy should be inoculated against Hardpad, Distemper, Hepatitis and Leptospirosis. This is usually done in two injections with fourteen days interval between them. Veterinary surgeons have slightly differing opinions about the age at which the puppy should be inoculated, so it is best to follow their advice. There is nothing worse than watching a dog die of

Distemper. Before vaccines were invented whole kennels would be infected, with every dog dying of the disease. So if you feel that the vets fee cannot be afforded then it is far better that you do not keep a dog. Remember that it is wise for the dog to have a booster injection once a year so the annual expense must be budgeted for.

## Grooming

Grooming is an essential part of dog ownership, which should be attended to daily. If it is treated as a game the dog is more likely to look forward to it rather than spending most of his time avoiding the brush or comb. Grooming a dog with the minimum of inconvenience will require a certain amount of control. To be able to put the dog in the stand, sit and down position, keeping him still just by the use of a couple of commands will facilitate a speedy job, but these are all training problems which are dealt with later.

There are many types of grooming products available at pet stores. The type of equipment to use really depends on the breed of dog and the nature of his coat. Good pet stores will advise on the suitability of your choice, but the authors have found that one of the most convenient is a brush in the form of a glove that fits over the hand. One side might have bristles on it, with the reverse being used for final polishing. A chromium plated metal comb is also very useful, but beware of the type that has sharp points which might scratch the dogs skin.

Unless absolutely necessary do not bath the dog, for this only destroys the natural oils of the coat. If he has been rolling in something unpleasant then there is little choice, but unlike humans bathing is not a prerequisite of canine cleanliness.

## Fleas

A dog can acquire fleas although living in a well kept clean house. The flea can be picked up by the dog from almost anywhere. They are not necessarily transferred from one dog to another, but although this does occur, the dog is more likely to acquire them from the hedgerows or fields. The flea is the host of the tapeworm so they should be dealt with at the first sign of infestation. Just because a dog is scratching himself does not mean that he has fleas. It can be just a skin irritation. However, if the scratching is excessive, inspect his coat carefully, paying particular attention to the area where his tail joins his body. The tiny black droppings of the flea are more likely to be spotted than the insect itself, so should signs of them be detected buy a flea powder or consult your veterinary surgeon who will supply the requisite product.

## Dog Fights and Animal Worrying

Dog fights do happen but although rarely fatal they need to be stopped quickly. We have already pointed out that two bitches living together are the most likely to fight to the death. Apart from stud dogs, two or more dogs will sometimes square up to each other for various reasons. It may be that their play has got out of hand or one is guarding his toy or bone, with the other trying to take it from him. Usually during such an argument one of the dogs will back down, becoming the under-dog. Often there is far more noise and gnashing of teeth than actual damage, which with well trained dogs can be stopped by a quick command of disapproval. A serious fight is best stopped by the use of a household broom which is ideal for separating the protagonists, but not readily available if out for a walk. One hears of advice such as pulling them out by their tails, but this is somewhat dangerous as the dog will think that the other one is causing this pain and turn round to bite what will probably be the hand or leg. If it is necessary to physically intervene between two fighters try to find an implement to separate them rather than risk damage to yourself.

Dogs that worry others, showing aggressive tendencies, are best stopped early in their lives. By wearing a training collar and lead they can be taken towards their fellow canines and at the first sign of trouble, given a hard sharp check with the lead plus a verbal command such as 'Leave'. This will have a two-fold affect. In all but the worst cases they will come to realise that such behaviour is unacceptable and also in time learn the meaning of the command, which can also be put to other uses. The correct use of the training collar and lead will be explained later, but dog training clubs are ideal for such training as the dog will quickly have to learn to live in peace with other canines.

Animal worrying is dealt with in a similar manner, but although on a lead it is not prudent to take an aggressive dog towards sheep, horses or cattle for the purpose of training unless the owners permission has been obtained.

Another thing to avoid is allowing your dog to chase birds. In the confines of the garden it may be quite funny to watch his hopeless attempts to catch them, but should he do so in the local recreation ground his chase of the bird may take him straight across the road with an accident or his death as a result.

# Chapter 4

# DOG TRAINING PRINCIPLES

## How a Dogs Mind Works

Before going into detail of training the dog to do any one thing it is essential that the reader understands the general principles involved. Before domesticated by man the dog was a wild animal that hunted and ran in a pack. The leader was usually a strong dominant male who commanded respect. For our purposes it is essential that the trainer becomes the pack leader no matter how strong willed is the dog under training. The disobedient unruly dog has assumed the position of pack leader in any household and has slotted each member into order beneath him. If the father of a family is the most dominant and also the dog trainer, the dog considers father to be number two in pack order, probably the mother is number three with the children following. Whilst it is preferable for one person to carry out the initial training, be it husband, wife or child, they should all understand the training principles and methods so that in the case of a family of four the dog knows he is number five in pack order. To achieve this state of affairs the trainer must always win any battle of will power. It is as simple as that.

Perhaps the most important point of all to know is that a dog only learns by the association of ideas. This applies to anything he is taught and also the bad habits that he acquires.

At a certain age it is possible to start to

vocally explain right and wrong to a young child but this is never possible with a dog. It is quite useless to correct or praise a dog for something he did thirty seconds or even hours ago, as he can only associate correction and reward with his immediate thoughts. Not only is it useless but the dog will become confused. In the case of correction, the confusion will cause apprehension which is to be avoided at all times. A classic example of this is the dog who is being walked in the woods or park who refuses to come back when called. Most unenlightened dog owners are guilty of teaching the dog not to come back under these circumstances. I am sure you would agree that one of the greatest pleasures in a dogs life is his walk, particularly when he is allowed to roam free from the restriction of the lead. If the dog is constantly called only to be placed on the lead ready to go home, he will associate coming when called with an unpleasant experience, namely the restriction of the lead and a curtailment of his enjoyment. Wise is the owner who makes a point of calling the dog, praising him when he arrives and then letting him run off again. By doing so the dog is not building up an unpleasant association of ideas but is finding that when he returns the praise received is pleasant. Even worse is the owner who has already fallen into this trap only to "compound the felony". After a lengthy time consuming spell of calling the dog without success, the owners temper rises and when the dog eventually returns because he is bored with what he is doing, he is chastised either verbally, physically or both. Now the last thing that the dog has done is to return. He is incapable of understanding that his owners wrath applies to something he should have done some time ago, in fact confusion sets in because he is not getting the expected reaction. In short he associates the idea of returning to his owner with displeasure so next time he is called he can almost be heard to say "not likely, I remember what happened last time I returned when called". So matters get worse and the owner becomes more exasperated as the dog appears to have become wilfully disobedient. But the owner has taught the dog to disobey, so the saying that "for every good dog there are a hundred bad owners" starts to appear very real indeed. Now this parable can be applied to all dog training whether it be house training or teaching walking to heel. Try to reason all problems yourself before taking hasty action remembering that the dog is incapable of doing so.

## Correction and Reward

All correction and reward must be instantaneous with the dogs immediate actions and not five seconds before or after. When this is understood dog training principles start to become a matter of common sense.

We have already discussed a dogs pleasure or displeasure associated with correction and reward, but it is essential that the reader understands how these four points are applied together. An obvious way of ensuring a pleasurable experience is to give food to the dog. There is nothing wrong in using tit-bits as an aid to training providing they are used sensibly and dispensed with as quickly as possible, but more of this later. The most satisfactory way of rewarding a dog is to praise him in a pleasant tone of voice using words such as "There's a good boy". However the words are unimportant and anything can be used as long as the sound is pleasant to the dog. Under certain circumstances the dog can be petted and stroked, which allied to the pleasant tone of voice also has the effect of imparting a sense of pleasure.

Displeasure is brought about by correction and many an old wives tale abounds on how this should be done. Forget beating with a stick, thrashing with the lead, hitting him over the nose with a rolled up newspaper and all the other ridiculous so called training methods. Not only are most of these cruel and usually carried out after the event but by virtue of the fact that the dog cannot reason, are useless and cause unnecessary apprehension. Now the apprehension of the dog may satisfy the owners having vented their temper on what is really a defenceless animal, but it has no use in good dog training and is to be abhorred. Correction under most circumstances should be a single word such as 'no' or 'aargh'. The word as such is unimportant, but what is essential is the tone of voice used to deliver it, which should be deep, slightly throaty and sharp. By using this tone the owner is acting in a manner which is understandable because it is similar to another dogs warning growl. This word 'no' can be used in degrees of sharpness and tone, varying from a nice warning to apparent displeasure on the part of the owner. Other forms of correction are the use of the training collar and lead in conjunction with a low tone of voice for definite misdemeanours, or in some initial training situations with a firm command. This is done by giving the lead a short sharp zip which must be gauged in relation to the size and age of the dog under training.

The most serious form of correction is to pick up the puppy or dog by the scruff of the neck, hold him close to the face and growl at him using words like 'What do you think you are doing'. A mother bitch would behave in a similar fashion to an erring puppy and therefore the trainer is using a method of correction understandable to the dog, but such corrections should only be used for definite disobedience. The owner must be certain that the dog knows better and it is not just a case of misunderstanding what is required of him. This severe correction should never be a daily occurrence, only being used in the most extreme circumstances at the split second the offence occurs as any time after that is too late. It cannot be over-stressed that the owner must be completely satisfied the puppy or dog has been wilfully disobedient, for many people confuse disobedience with their own inability to communicate to the dog the way he should behave. Should a trainer make this mistake then further confusion in the dogs mind will be the result, and confusion only leads to apprehension.

All these forms of correction are designed to impart displeasure just as food, praise and patting give a sense of pleasure. Used correctly they are the substitutes for the inability to reason with him.

## Sounds and Commands

Many are the experienced dog trainers who have been asked "What are the magic words used to train a dog?" The words are of course unimportant in themselves and those normally used are because they suit the impression the trainer wishes to impart to the dog. For instance 'There's a good dog' is much easier to say in a pleasant tone than in a gruff voice. The trainer could say 'Fiddlesticks' instead of 'No', but bye-standers would think this a little strange. The tone together with the sound used are the most important factors, so we must consider which words should be used as commands or requests. We loosely refer to all dog training words as commands, but many should be used as requests.

The words introduced into a dog's vocabulary should be short so that they are explicit. For good domestic control of the pet dog they should be kept to a minimum, thus avoiding any unnecessary confusion. The first requirement is for the dog to understand his name followed by words to show that we are pleased such as 'Good Dog'. Once any other form of training is commenced other words become necessary that will cover most requirements. 'Come', 'Heel', 'Sit', should be used as requests, whilst 'No', 'Leave', 'Down', 'Stay' and 'Wait' all requiring instant response, are better considered as commands. For simplicity, from here on this book will refer to both requests and commmands by the latter word as this is the normal practise to describe dog training terms. A dog well trained to respond to these seven words will be perfectly under control without being a liability to anyone while the handler is present. The only additional word might be the command 'Fetch' should this be a requirement for your pet, but a useful training aid is a short phrase to indicate to the dog that he is no longer required and the training session has finished. Phrases such as 'That'll do' or 'Off you go', once understood will help to avoid any such confusion, allowing him to realise that he is free to go his own way. Such a release phrase becomes useful at other times to signify that he is not required or is in the way, so without worrying too much about implicit obedience the phrase should be used consistently, then the dog will come to understand the meaning.

All words used as requests or commands should be constant in tone and pitch but they must have consistent meanings. If the words 'Get Down' are used to stop the dog jumping up or to remove him from the furniture, it will be most confusing to use 'Down' to indicate that he should be in that position.

Another good example is that a child is generally told to sit or lie down but in dog training we either want the dog to "sit" or "down" and must consistantly use both of these words on their own to convey the requirement without confusion. The trainer must never get into the habit of what we term "begging the dog" to respond. Unless a command is immediately obeyed a verbal command alone should not be given a second time without the accompanying training aid to ensure that he obeys and must always react instantly. The mistake that so many people make is to keep repeating the command without using the aid when immediate response is not forthcoming, hence they fall into the trap of allowing the dog to obey only when it suits him.

## Training Equipment

Good equipment is important for safety and to do the requisite job. A collar is essential, but leather or nylon collars with buckles are not suitable for training, neither are all the fancy collars that look nice on the dog but will not serve any training purpose. One of the myths about dog training is the collar that is used. This is a chain formed by welded links which can be purchased in various lengths and link sizes, usually erroneously referred to as a choke chain. A more correct name for it is a check chain or training collar, but if you ask for the latter in a shop they will probably not know what you require. The fault lies with the manufacturers of this type of training equipment many of whom still catalogue them as choke chains, hence the shop orders and sells by this name. The links of a training collar should be approximately the size of the small finger nail but this will vary according to the size of the dog. The very thin linked chain more like a necklace should be avoided even with small breeds, for this will only cut into the dogs neck. The other extreme is the large oval linked chain such as that favoured by the police for their German Shepherd Dogs (Alsatians). Such a chain is clumsy and does not have the same quick response as the smaller links when moved by the lead. The action we require is similar to that of a zip being closed quickly, and strangely the sound the chain will make is not all that dissimilar. There is a definite difference to a jerk of the chain as opposed to a zip, so when reference is made to a zip the reader will understand what we wish to convey.

The length of the training collar should just be large enough to fit over the dogs head without any force. A collar which is too long will inhibit good training, also being dangerous should the dog catch his paws through the loose part hanging round his neck. One word of warning about these collars is that they are better taken off when the dog is not under supervision in case of such an accident.

Many types of leads can be purchased in various qualities. To be avoided like the plague are the imitation or cheap leather type, generally not very substantial in thickness and often only having one small rivet supposedly securing a clip which is better described as a piece of bent wire. They are usually the cheapest and certainly the most dangerous should they break whilst walking the dog.

If a pedigree dog has been purchased he will have cost a lot of money so it is wise to spend a little more on good equipment. A chain lead is strong, ideal for tying the dog who will not be able to chew through it to get away, but they are hard on the hands for training purposes. Plaited leads do not have the necessary flexibility no matter how expensive, and usually have an inferior clip attached.

The correct training lead is one that has been with us for many years. It chould be 3'6'' to 4'0'' in length made from good quality bridle leather. The thickness should be reasonable for the size of the dog to be trained, but even for small dogs should not be too thin. There should be a handle at one end and a good quality bolt action trigger hook on a swivel secured to the opposite end. The handle and the hook should be well stitched and can also have a rivet for extra safety. Such a lead treated regularly with one of the various brands of leather preservative sold by a saddler, will last a lifetime. Maybe the stitches will need to be renewed after some years, but careful attention will pay dividends.

### Wearing the Training Collar and Lead

There are two ways of putting the training collar on the dog. One such way will mean that it will operate as a choke, which is absolutely useless for training purposes and somewhat cruel. The links of the chain should be allowed to drop through one of the two large rings found at each end. The owner should stand facing the dog holding the chain so that it forms a figure six lying on its front, with the loop of the six in the right hand and the spare chain in the left. It should be slipped over the dogs head to form a training collar, with the ring that the links run through on the left side of the neck. Once the chain is on the dog if it has the appearance of a figure six lying on its back it is upside down thereby acting as a choke, so it must be taken off to be replaced the correct way round. The collar once correctly worn will tighten when the handler zips the lead, slackening of its own accord as soon as the zip is finished. With the lead attached to the large ring

*Preparing the training collar*

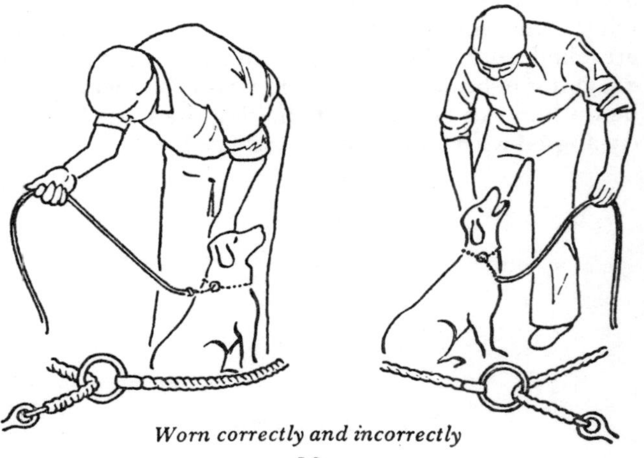

*Worn correctly and incorrectly*

at the end of the chains tail it will be possible to quickly correct the dog. The degree of zip used must be determined by the owner who should take account of the size and nature of the dog under training. If applied correctly, simultaneously with a command, the dog will respond and should immediately be praised for doing so.

It is wrong to assume that the training collar will automatically cure all, it has to be used correctly and with sympathy. It must never be used for continually nagging the dog but rather only when necessary, ensuring an immediate response.

Eventually when the lead is given a zip, the sound of the links running against the ring of the chain will induce a reaction from the dog prior to the chain becoming tight.

Later chapters will describe the use of the training collar for individual exercises, but before any training is attempted with this equipment the dog should be allowed on several occasions to run free whilst wearing it. This will allow him to become accustomed to the collar without it being an irritant. Once this has been achieved the lead can be attached so that he can again run free with the lead dragging behind him. At such times the owner must be on hand to ensure that the dog does not become entangled with a bush or any other object.

# Chapter 5

# EDUCATING THE PUPPY

## Responding to His Name

Having chosen a name for the puppy, teaching the recognition of his name can begin from the first time he is fed. A recall is formally taught later, but as an aid to an immediate response, a pleasant sound that will always be associated with pleasure, can be used each time the puppy is fed. Nothing is more pleasant to the average puppy than feeding

*Teaching the recognition of his name*

time, therefore such a sound will have an association of pleasure throughout his life. This sound should be soft in tone, and whilst the sound in itself is immaterial, a shushing sound rather like steam escaping from a kettle is ideal. By using this sound interspersed with the puppy's name several objectives are quickly achieved. The puppy learns his name, the meaning of the sound, and will always rush to you when he hears them. It really is very simple, consuming no more time than it takes to feed the little bundle of fun. When the time comes to take recall training a stage further this sound can be used in conjunction with a tit-bit. If only all breeders would use such a method every time food is taken to the litter of puppies, it would be a simple matter for the new owners to copy the sound thus taking home a puppy already partly trained. Alas the world is not perfect so it is unlikely that you will have purchased from such an enlightened breeder, however all is far from lost, just start this education at the first feeding time and continue for several months or for ever.

### Teaching the Puppy to Come

It is as well to establish at this point when the dog's name should be used during training. It is the opinion of the authors that the name used in conjunction with a command, is best reserved for when the dog is required to come towards his handler. Never mix the dog's name with other commands, for it must be remembered that if the advice previously given is followed, he will associate his name with returning to his handler. For example if the name preceeds the command 'Stay' the handler is risking confusion by asking the dog to come and to stay at the same time.

After a while the puppy will be responding to his

*Teaching the puppy to come*

name interspersed with the pleasant sound, rushing towards you when hearing them thus making it possible to take the training a little further. To do so put the puppy on a lead, and holding it in the right hand, walk forward with him on your left side. Immediately you are both doing so, suddenly start walking slowly backwards simultaneously calling his name, which being associated with pleasure, will turn the dog towards you. This will achieve two objectives, the fact that he will come when he hears his name is being consolidated and his attention is being gained, which is a response that is very important. Do not forget to praise this response, adding if you wish that interesting sound which in itself is a method of imparting pleasure to the puppy.

## Teaching the Puppy to Sit

Having reached the preceding stage, the first lessons in learning to sit on command can become part of the sequence. As the puppy approaches draw the right hand which is holding the lead towards the chest, this will have the effect of lifting the puppy's head while simultaneously the left hand gently presses his rear into a sitting position. At the same time as this is done, give the command 'Sit' followed by praise as the puppy responds. The praise should not be overdone to the extent that he jumps up in joy, but should be sufficient to let him know he has done well. This sequence is called "applying the three aids", the right hand lifting the lead, the left hand pressing down on his hind quarters, combined with the command 'Sit'.

Bearing in mind that on many occasions the puppy will have been fondled by the hands, it is quite possible that he will try to nibble them or jump up, so they must be kept still. At all times when teaching a puppy the handler must be conscious of the hands, which must be moved smoothly but slowly and never waved about. This also applies to the bending of the body which will be necessary to place the puppy in the sitting position. As soon as he is still, very slowly move either or both hands to gently fondle his head without allowing him to move. As the name and the pleasant sound have always had an association with food, now is the time to give him a little tit-bit. This gentle teaching session can be repeated several times taking care that he does not become bored. After a few days it will be found that he will come when he hears his name and the sound, so it will be a simple matter to call him then slip the training collar over his head without having to catch him first.

### Exposing the Puppy to Noise and Traffic

Unfortunately most puppies are born into an environment of quiet home life. It is therefore advisable, that to ensure they do not grow up to be afraid of sudden noises, some action is taken to gradually expose them to every day sounds. It has to be borne in mind that the puppy should not be taken for walks until he has been inoculated, which will be twelve to fourteen weeks of age. Much can be done prior to this time and one way is to create noises while preparing the puppy's food or whilst he is eating it. A tin can be kicked or two pieces of wood banged together with little fear of apprehension from the puppy, for he will be more intent on the pleasure of his food than the noise. Build up such noises gradually rather than on the first occasion holding a dustbin lid over his head whilst banging it with a stick, for such irresponsible action could have the opposite effect.

When the puppy is still small he can be carried out to the road to become accustomed to the noise and smell of traffic. Holding him in your arms stand well back on the pavement, choosing a not too busy street at first, then as the traffic passes talk to him and gently assure him that all is well. As he becomes accustomed to these strange objects hurtling by, busier streets can be chosen. By the time his immunisation period has passed and he has been walked along the pavement on several occasions with you between him and the traffic, even a large articulated lorry passing will not trouble him. Whatever you do he must not be thrown in at the deep end by being taken to the middle of a busy town on his first outing as this will only frighten him.

*Exposing the puppy to noise and traffic*

## Ensuring the Puppy Respects You

It is important to establish at an early age that the puppy understands his handler is the leader. If he doesn't respect your authority while young, once he grows to a full size dog it will be extremely difficult to persuade him that you are number one and not him. This is easily achieved during his first few weeks at home by ensuring that his food and toys can be taken away from him without objection, that playing with him doesn't turn into puppy biting, and that the handler always wins any battle of wits. It is purely a question of establishing that in the pack order there is no chance of him becoming the leader. If he does, then later training will have to become more a question of corrective measures rather than the puppy being channelled in the right direction from an early age.

*Taking food away from the puppy*

## Travel Sickness

The motor car is a part of modern day life that is here to stay. It is unlikely that it will never be necessary to take the dog out in a car, in fact the reverse will be more probable. The way a dog reacts to car travel and his general behaviour connected with the car, is a most important part of modern dog training that cannot be overlooked. It is surprising just how many people expect the dog to instinctively be the perfect passenger without giving any thought to introducing him to the car gradually. Much of the problem of canine car sickness can be attributed to a lack of foresight on the part of the owner, although like humans, not every dog will be subject to this complaint. The constant swaying motion of the car particularly at the rear, and the traffic rushing by can cause this problem. A dog likely to be a candidate for car sickness would do best to travel as near as possible to the gear lever for this is the area that has the least amount of swaying movement. Whilst it is quite amusing to see a dog sitting on the front passenger seat seemingly master of all he surveys, the best place for him would be tied in the well in front of this seat. In such a position he will not be able to see the passing traffic nor will there be so much sideways movement. It is always difficult to find a suitable place to tie the dog and anything attached to the door is unsuitable. Far better to have a small ring fixed to the side of the front passenger well where he can be easily tied, allowing you to get in and out of the vehicle without disturbing him.

If the dog does suffer from sickness it is unwise to feed him prior to commencing a journey, or to let him drink too much any time that you stop for exercise or food.

## Car Training

The ideal vehicle for a dog is an estate car so that he can travel in the back without being in anyones way or leaving his hairs to adhere to clothing. Not everyone favours this type of car, so without rear door access the best place for a dog is in the front passenger well. In either case a puppy should learn how to get in and out of the car and how to behave himself once inside. This is best taught in the driveway to your house where it will be possible to open the car door then take the puppy on the lead towards it. Upon reaching the open door sit the puppy in front of it, forestalling any of his attempts to get in until told to do so. This might seem a little strange, but a dog regularly taken out in the car can be so eager to get in that he will pull you off your feet, or leap on to the seats damaging articles that would have been better moved first. After waiting a

*Car Training*

few seconds encourage him in, or if necessary lift him in, then place him in the down position tieing him so that he is comfortable but cannot get up. If there is any resistance a little soothing will soon calm him down. If the puppy is very young it is unlikely that he will have been taught to go down on command, so a little help will be necessary. After a short while untie him, but wait a few seconds before inviting him to get out or he will soon associate untieing with what follows, making it difficult for you to release him. The act of getting out of the car is probably the most important, for when wishing to disembark the dog in a busy street it must be on command and not before. If he attempts to leap out it will be necessary to restrain him from doing so until perfectly certain that he is steady and that you are in a position to control him on the lead as he alights. This can be repeated several times with the door left open until he has accepted the situation sufficiently to enable the door to be shut while he is left inside for a few minutes. The next stage is best carried out with an assistant to start the engine, but leave the car stationary while you sit inside soothing the puppy. After several sessions of going through each sequence up to this stage, next ask the assistant to drive the car whilst you are left free to attend the puppy. In such a way car manners can be taught to him, so as he grows up he will be unlikely to embarrass you with his ill behaviour or cause an accident.

Although at a later stage it is hoped that the dog will respond to the command 'Down', always keep him tied so that there is no fear of him being a nuisance in any way. Dog guards are available to fit most makes of estate car but these are best not fitted until such a time as it is no longer necessary for you to reach the dog for purposes of car training.

# Chapter 6

## WALKING TO HEEL

### (Heelwork)

One of the greatest problems the average dog owner faces is to teach the dog to walk closely to heel without pulling on the lead. Many young dogs are extremely boisterous, intent on walking where they wish. This behaviour creates problems for the owner of a small dog and becomes multiplied many times over when the dog is of medium to large size. Some dog owners simply give up taking the dog for a walk or erroneously allow him to walk on a road where he wishes without the lead attached. A dog needs his daily exercise and should not be a nuisance or a danger when he is out with his owner. Untrained dogs will pull forward, to the side or walk across the owner, and the lead will often become entangled with the dogs legs or those of his handler.

The first thing we have to establish is the correct position for the dog when at heel. It is generally accepted practice throughout the world that the dog should always be on the left side of the handler. Many theories are advanced as to why the left is the chosen side. It is not the intention of this book to go into such detail, suffice it to say that if training a dog to walk on the right he will be the odd one out. Having established which side of the handler the dog should walk we must now determine the correct position in relation to the leg. It is generally accepted that the dogs neck should be level with the leg of the person walking him, and that he should not be more than three or four inches to the side of the leg.

If training a puppy, once he is three months of age he will have had his final inoculation and the owner will want to take him out for exercise. To forestall the puppy getting into bad habits, it is preferable that just prior to this time he has been taught the correct position for walking to heel. If he is taken out before this lesson has been learned he may already have developed such habits as pulling on the lead or walking wide, associating the lead as a licence to walk just how he wants to. This is of course undesirable, so it is far better to teach the correct postion before these ideas become fixed in his mind. To teach heelwork it is necessary to establish a basic principle that each time the handler steps off with the dog three things must consistently happen, always in the correct order. The first is that the dog's name should be used to gain his attention, immediately followed by the command "Heel", then finally the handler should step off with the left foot. In dog training classes this is sometimes referred to as "one, two, three", and it is quite amazing how often the handler forgets, starting off with three followed by one and two. It should be obvious that fractionally before stepping off, the dog will need an indication of what is required. So try to keep it in mind that "one" is the dogs name "two" is the command "Heel", with "three" being the step off with the left foot. The reader may well wonder why they must set off with the left foot as opposed to either foot. Dogs are very aware of any body movements that a handler may make consciously or unconsciously, therefore we can make use of this awareness by consistently using the left leg to commence heelwork training. The left leg is preferred to the right as it is nearest to the dog having an effect of drawing him forward. Stepping off with the right leg can then be reserved for teaching the dog to stay or to wait until called.

Assuming the dog has been allowed to run free wearing a training collar with the lead attached and it is no longer an irritant, heelwork training can commence by placing the dog on the left side in the heel position. Hold the lead by the handle with the right hand, gathering the excess into folds in the same hand until approximately nine inches of slack lead loops across the body of the dog.

Teaching the dog his correct heel position is best achieved by walking gently in large left circles. Using the "one, two, three" method give the dog's name followed by the command "Heel", then step off with the left leg doing these three things within the space of a second but in the correct order. Whenever he moves ahead, stop and gently bring him back to the correct position with the use of the command "Heel" simultaneously running the left hand down the lead to ease him back into place. If after many attempts he still persists with pulling, or if training an older dog that has already acquired such a bad habit and pulls incessantly, let him get ahead, release the lead tension, then give a hard sharp check at the same time using the command "Heel". It is very important that as soon as this has been done the lead tension is released allowing the training collar to slacken while immediate praise is given. It is usually only necessary to take this course of action once or twice, especially with puppies. However, with an older dog that has always been allowed to pull on the lead he cannot be deterred by correcting just once or twice, it is usually necessary to check such a dog hard several times and over several training sessions before he realises the futility of his actions. These methods also apply to the dog

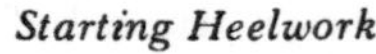

*Starting Heelwork*

*Stepping off*

*Easing him back to heel*

*Checking the older dog that pulls*

who insists on pulling violently away to the side. This form of correction is not cruel, it being more of a kindness to stop the dog spending the rest of his life pulling and straining with saliva frothing from his mouth. All this can be over and done with in a few days if the method described is accurately carried out.

At this stage of a puppy or adult dog's training it is unusual for him to hang back in a manner described as "lagging" as this is more likely to be found in the dog that has been under training for some time. Due to incorrect timing of the lead correction plus the command, or constant unnecessary nagging on the lead by the handler, the dog has become apprehensive of the lead, the command "Heel", and everything he associates with heelwork training. Should this happen, then before trying any more heel training read this chapter and

*Walking in a left circle*

the chapter on dog training principles again, think the problem through then start at the beginning again using far more encouragement without any lead correction.

Occasionally when first attempting to walk a dog with a lead, particularly a young one, he will put his behind on the ground and refuse to budge. In these circumstances just walk to the end of the lead and when it is reached continue walking calmly and gently, ignoring the dog who will be forced to either get up and walk or be dragged in the sitting position. As soon as he ceases to resist by getting to his feet, encourage him to your left side by vocal praise whilst drawing him close with the lead.

Once the dog understands the meaning of the command "Heel" and knows his position, continue walking in a left circle but step up the pace so that it becomes a slightly brisk walking pace. At this stage the lead can be carried in either hand but not in both hands at the same time, and something that interests the dog can be held in the free hand to maintain his attention. Whilst the pace of the handler should be reasonable, the length of each pace should be kept short, with the dog receiving plenty of encouragement at all times. Phrases such as "there's a good boy" used in a pleasant tone will show the dog that he is doing right, but do not fall into the trap of praising just because this book says so. Take the opportunity to praise when the dog is correct and not when he is wrong, or he will never learn and it will not be his fault. As he gains confidence the encouragement can be dropped to a whisper which will make him pay attention. Excessive voice volume does not necessarily have the effect of making the dog work better, in fact the opposite is often the case. If he jumps up during early heel training do not worry for unfortunately some breeds, and particularly the larger built dogs, will all too soon become bored and slow, so while the excitement is there encourage it. Walk at a pace that is comfortable and never make the mistake of slowing down or speeding up to suit the dog for then he will be in charge of the proceedings and not you.

So far we have not discussed sitting the dog in the heel position during heelwork lessons. This is a deliberate omission for at this stage the dog is only just learning to enjoy walking on a slack lead. An additional exercise will only make confusion in the dogs mind more likely, and confusion will lead to apprehension, with lagging being the possible end result. Imagine being told to dig a hole then fill it in, with the whole rigmarole being repeated time and time again. If added to this, each time one is asked to get in and out of the hole without any explanation of such a performance, confusion would be a logical end product. In the dogs case, if one minute he is being asked to walk and the next minute he is told to sit, the result is the same. Sitting during heelwork is best taught once the dog is becoming proficient, and then it should be taught as a separate exercise. For this reason we will deal with it in the following chapter.

Once the dog will confidently walk at heel in a left circle, that circle can become more oblong so that two sides of it are straight, with the bends becoming left wheels whilst his attention is maintained.

All that has been said so far has probably taken many training sessions to achieve, with each session being kept to ten minutes or less if the dog looks like becoming bored. Progression through each stage of training is necessarily slow, with the handler never making the mistake of moving on to something more difficult until the previous stage has been happily mastered by the dog and with confidence. Assuming

*The right turn* *The about turn*

that such is the case, the next stage is for the handler to walk in lines which bend first to one side and then to the other, rather as though walking through a slalom course.

Slowly change the right wheels into right turns, but it must be a gradual progression to a full 90 degrees, for to go straight into such a sharp turn can be another cause of lagging. The right turn is best taught first, followed by the logical progression of teaching the about turn. Once the dog will execute a right turn without going wide, this turn can then include a further right wheel which can gradually become an about turn. It sometimes happens that the dog tends to go wide on these two turns. This is usually caused by his inattention to the lesson, and such wide turns will eventually develop into a bad habit unless the dog is corrected immediately the fault develops. The answer is to give a short sharp zip on the lead simultaneously giving the command "Heel", but this must be done at the first indication of a wide turn rather than when the dog is three-quarters of the way through it. Immediately he has corrected the turn the handler should praise him, thus he will learn what is right and what is wrong.

The left turn is the last one to be taught to the dog. It will only be confusing if the handler turns straight into the dog possibly kicking him in the

*The left turn*

process. The lead can be of assistance by holding it in the right hand while using the left hand as a funnel to run it through, thus guiding the dog round in a loop before completing the turn. The command "Heel" can be given as this manoeuvre commences, with praise being remembered when the dog responds in the required manner.

So far no mention has been made of the posture

and attitude of the handler. At all times during heelwork training, walk in an upright manner without stooping or bending towards the dog. It is possible to see without bending what the dog is doing, also the lead will transmit much information about his activity or lack of it. If the handler finds this impossible or the dog under training is very small, incline the head slightly towards him whilst keeping the body upright. Many people bend unnaturally over the dog when practising turns. This is quite unnecessary, is likely to teach the dog to make a wide turn, and looks extremely untidy. After all the object of all this is to be able to walk the dog along the road making turns where necessary whilst he remains in the correct position. The owner who is bent over the dog is going to look somewhat strange to other people.

### Without the lead

To teach the dog to walk at heel without the lead attached is really a matter of perfecting heelwork with the use of the lead. When confident that he fully understands what is required, responding to every manoeuvre, then and only then is heelwork without the lead attempted. At this stage it is advisable to step up the amount of encouragement to subsitute for the lack of control that the lead gives. A trap to avoid is using too much encouragement or praise to the extent that it all becomes a ceaseless drone that means nothing to the dog. Should he stray more than fractionally from the heel position he is not yet ready for lead free training, so the handler must immediately revert to lead training, trying again at a later date. Even if the dog responds well to walking at heel without the lead, it is a mistake to continually train in this fashion, far better to continue heelwork with the lead attached for at least 80% of the time. It may well be that after training your dog will walk at heel in a perfect manner without the lead. If this is the case never show off your training powers by walking the dog without a lead on the streets. The dog has not yet been born that will not leave the handlers side under any circumstances, so never allow him the opportunity to do so or you may risk the possibility of a traffic accident. At all times dogs must be kept on a lead anywhere there is a remote possibility of traffic.

Take time, care and patience with heelwork training, always reverting to the previous stage if the dog is uncertain. Doing so will help to ensure that your dog is admired for his good behaviour whilst walking to heel.

*Heelwork — the end product*

## Reminders

1. Allow the dog to become accustomed to the training collar before commencing training.
2. Ensure the training collar is the right way round.
3. Allow approximately nine inches of slack lead.
4. "One, two, three," dogs name, 'Heel,' step off.
5. Always commence by moving the left leg first.
6. Walk in large left circles.
7. If he pulls ahead gently bring him back to heel.
8. If a check is necessary praise must follow.
9. Do not incorporate sits during initial heel training.
10. Use more encouragement for a dog that lags, correction is useless.
11. Praise frequently when the dog is right but don't overdo it.
12. Progress from left circles to bends then to turns.
13. The left turn is the last to teach the dog.
14. Keep the training sessions short and interesting, little and often is best.
15. Revert to lead training if the dog is unsure of heelwork without the lead.
16. Always keep the dog on a lead when in a street.
17. Never rush heelwork training, but progress with care and patience.

# Chapter 7

# TEACHING THE SIT, DOWN AND STAY

## The Sit

It is probably true to say that the average pet dog owner will use the command 'Sit' for his dog more frequently than the other words in his vocabulary. Apart from the obvious uses of the command for a well trained dog, the sit becomes very useful for controlling the dog at the beginning, the end and sometimes during other training exercises. For example, to be able to sit the dog at heel on command becomes an aid to advising him that he will need to pay attention as he is about to be controlled. Bearing this in mind it is therefore good strategy that a controlled sit should be achieved at an early stage in the dogs training.

The sit at heel is very often taught as part of heelwork training. Whilst there is nothing wrong with this, it is preferable to leave the sit out of early heelwork lessons as continual stopping and starting only serves to add confusion before the dog really understands the meaning of the command 'Heel'. However, as described in the previous chapter, there will probably have been times when it was necessary to guide the dog back to heel by running the left hand down the lead to ease him into the correct position. As with puppy training this routine can be varied by the handler allowing the dog to go to the

*Teaching the sit in front*

end of the lead which should be held in the right hand. As he reaches the leads length give it a light flick using the command 'Come' while commencing to walk backwards. When the dog arrives in front of you, stop and quickly lean forward to tap his backside with the hand while saying 'Sit', but do not overdo this or the dog will sit well away to avoid the tap. A visible 'tit-bit' held in the hand is an aid to this exercise for it encourages the dog towards you, plus by drawing both hands to the chest he will no doubt be looking up to watch them, which can help straighten his body prior to being placed into the sit.

Whether you wish to insist on straight sits is entirely up to the individual. By straight sits we mean a dog sitting with his backbone straight rather than at an angle to his handler. A straight sit at heel would mean that the dogs backbone was parallel to the handlers legs. It is just as easy to teach a dog to sit straight as it is to teach him to sit crooked, however if you only wish to teach domestic obedience to the dog it matters not at what angle he sits. It may be that later you will join a dog training club with the intention of competing. In competition marks are lost for crooked sits, which are more difficult to correct than to never let the dog sit crooked during early training. From the point of view that the choice is yours, this book will refer to the dog sitting straight, but such fastidiousness can be ignored by the reader.

The dog can also be taught to sit at heel which is best accomplished whilst walking him in the heel position. To teach the dog to sit in front of the handler we have described the use of "the three aids" which are also used for the sit at heel in the same manner. The right hand holds the lead tight

*Teaching the sit at heel*

above the dogs head which keeps the front half of him steady, while the left hand is placed on his rear to press him into the sit, simultaneously giving the command. To accomplish this manoeuvre there is a choice of bending the trunk forwards or backwards. Bending forwards will bring the handlers head over the dog, which in good dog training is to be avoided whenever possible. Always bend the trunk of the body backwards when pressing the dog into the sit at heel position. By the use of the three aids it becomes necessary for the dog to put his bottom on the ground which is exactly what is required. This is likely to be at any angle to the handler unless, by the use of the right hand holding the lead and the left hand on his hindquarters, he is guided as well as pressed into a straight sit. Immediately the dog responds he must be praised to indicate that he is doing what is required. This routine must be practised repeatedly over the course of several days or even weeks, until the raising of the right hand plus the movement of the left towards his rear becomes sufficient for a response every time the command 'Sit' is given. Eventually these two latter aids can be dispensed with, but beware of expecting the dog to be a quick learner by leaving out the aids altogether just because he has sat once or twice without this compulsion. The handler who does so very soon becomes one who has to repeat the command several times before there is any likelihood of obedience. It is far better to continually use all the aids until absolutely certain that there is little chance of anything but immediate response by the dog.

Assuming that the dog will now sit at heel understanding the meaning of the command and is able to walk on a slack lead, then already considerable control has been achieved. Not only is he becoming more manageable, but the handler is in a position to teach other very important exercises which are better commenced from a controlled start, such as sitting in the heel position.

## The Down

The ability to instantly put the dog in the down position by the use of one promptly obeyed command is generally referred to as "the immediate down" which is perhaps the most essential part of any dogs training. Whilst most other training exercises well executed are pieces of the jig-saw that go to make a well trained dog, the ability to drop him instantly, be he by your side or some distance away, can save injury or even death. If all other parts of a dogs training only meet with partial success, this exercise must be practised until perfect. Although precautions will have been taken to ensure that the dog is controlled by the lead where there is any likelihood of traffic, things can go wrong, such as a broken lead. The dog may well rush towards a busy road or even be half way across it, but calling him to you might be just as dangerous as letting him continue. The answer might well be to drop the dog, for doing so should result in his instant inactivity.

Before attempting to teach the dog to go down on command at a distance, it is necessary to perfect an instant reaction to the command whilst he is by your side. The first point to realise is that during the first few lessons the majority of dogs struggle against the handlers attempts to place them in the down. Being a compulsive form of training this is a natural reaction which gradually lessons as the dog begins to understand what is required. It may well be the handlers instinct to praise or soothe the dog whilst he is objecting to going down, but this will not help him to learn quickly. Whilst he is resisting, the handler must be firm with the voice and ensure that the dogs struggles do not result in him winning, for if he gets the idea that his resolve is greater than the handlers his resistance will only be prolonged.

One method of teaching the dog to go down is to place him in the sit position at heel. Stand across the dog at a slight angle, holding the lead in the right hand so that it is looped nearly touching the floor between the dog and the right hand. With the left foot positioned as high up the lead and as near the dogs neck as possible, put the left foot firmly to the ground whilst taking the pressure of the lead with the right hand. As this is done the command 'Down' should be given in a firm low authoritative manner.

*Four stages of down training*

If this is smartly carried out it may be possible to catch the dog unawares so that there is no resistance, or alternatively continued pressure may need to be applied to the lead by the foot until he goes down. In either case once he is down keep the foot on the lead, stroke the dogs head with the left hand whilst using a pleasant tone of voice to tell him how clever he is. If the dog wriggles keep the foot firmly in place holding the lead secured to the ground whilst repeating the command. At any time the dog stops struggling, immediately praise him. Slowly it will be found that the lead pressure can be released until it is possible to lay it out on the ground, gradually moving away from the dog.

An alternative method of teaching the down can be used by holding the lead handle in the right hand whilst quickly sliding the left hand down the lead until it reaches the training collar. Immediately this happens, the handler should compel the dog to the ground by holding the lead firmly where it joins the training collar until lead and hand reach the floor, while the handler drops to the left knee to avoid bending over the dog. Once any struggles have ceased the left foot can be used to hold the lead which will free the left hand to stroke the dog whilst he is praised. Gradually stand up, continuing the praise providing that he remains inactive.

As in the previously described method, once the dog is steady the lead can be laid on the ground whilst the handler gradually moves away, retaining a certain degree of control by keeping the left foot on it. With both methods the act of compelling the dog to the ground will have to be repeated several times, probably over several training sessions. At any time the dog is responding of his own accord, the pressure on the lead with the foot or the hand can be

*Alternative four stages of down training*

slackened to give him the chance to go down without assistance. When this happens immediate praise should be given, reverting to lead pressure plus a repeat command should he change his mind by resisting again. Gradually the action of the left foot or left hand can just become signals additional to the command, as they are no longer necessary for compulsion but remain effective as signals to help the dog to understand.

Until the dog sitting by your side will consistantly go down the instant the command is given and without any signals being necessary, no attempt should be made to drop him at a distance. The further away from his handler the less submissive the dog becomes, so it is essential that the process of getting an immediate down at a distance is a gradual, careful build up. One way of doing this is to run with the dog attached to the lead giving the command 'Down' while ensuring that this new innovation is obeyed by the use of the lead by either hand or foot. Gradually it should be possible to carry this out with the dog responding a full leads length away, but a clever dog will soon start to anticipate what is required if it is done too often in one training session.

When attempting the immediate down without the lead the dog may not respond as he thinks that he is no longer under control. Therefore, to be certain that there will be an instant response at a distance of two or three feet, it is better to start the lead free training by the side of the dog, never moving progressively away unless he is responding instantly. At no time during the down training should the handler give a second command without compelling the dog to obey.

From the first attempt to teach the dog the

*Teaching the dog to go down at a distance*

meaning of the command 'Down' to the perfect immediate down at a distance, will probably take several weeks to achieve. Be patient, ensure each degree of difficulty is carried out with perfection and then you will be the owner of a dog that can always be controlled even though it may only be to stop him in his tracks.

## Reminders

1. Do not teach the sit during early heelwork lessons.

2. Don't hope the dog will sit, use "the three aids".

3. Continual bending over the dog to place him in the sit will make him sit wide.

4. Never give a second command without taking action to ensure it is obeyed.

5. Praise the dog when he responds to the command.

6. Make training sessions little and often.

7. The immediate down can save lives.

## The Stay

The Stay is the word used to indicate that the dog is required to stop where he has been left until the handler returns. Of all the exercises taught to the dog this is the only one that requires total inactivity. It would therefore seem that to teach him to stay would be extremely simple but nothing could be further from the truth. Dogs are inquisitive animals used to investigating noises and movements that interest them. Added to this is the problem of the dog trainer making life very confusing for the dog by asking him to stop still one minute, only to call him the next. Knowledgeable dog trainers fully understand this problem. By making a distinct difference between the commands and signals when leaving a dog to be subsequently called, and the command that is used if the intention is to return to him, they avoid confusion. When practising calling the dog it will sometimes be necessary to leave him in either the sit or the down position. Prior to leaving him by all means use the command 'Sit' or 'Down' with the word 'Wait' as an optional extra, however never use the word 'Stay' if you want to own a dog reliable to this command. Reserve this word to be used only when requiring him to stop whilst you go away, always returning to his side before releasing him. It is also unwise to practise a stay exercise prior to, or immediately after, a recall. By adhering to these rules help is being given to the dog who will find it a lot easier to understand what is required.

To commence teaching this exercise place the dog in the sit position holding the lead in the right hand. Use the command 'Sit Stay' simultaneously giving a signal with the left hand by placing the flat of the hand a few inches in front of his nose. Taking a pace

*Four stages of stay training*

slightly to the right of the dog, use the left hand as a funnel on the lead running it straight up from the top of the dogs neck until it is held reasonably tight, approximately eighteen inches above his head. Move round to face him in front of his nose repeating the command 'Sit Stay', then slightly lower the left hand to loosen the tension on the lead. If the dog makes any attempt to move, the left hand must immediately apply the slight tension, having the effect of lifting the head and making movement impossible while the command is repeated firmly. Once he ceases his attempts to move, gently praise him and slightly slacken the lead, returning to his side after a few seconds. The amount of praise must not be over-done or the dog will be incited to move. A golden rule of stay training is to never overdo the length of time that the dog is left, for a five second stay successfully achieved will be progress, while a 30 second attempt with the dog moving at 29 seconds is retrograde training. Stay training is really a question of building the dogs confidence to stop where he is without the desire to go to the handler whether he is in or out of sight. During this early training a stay of 15 seconds is quite sufficient, which might seem a ludicrously short time but to a dog new to stay training it is probably an eternity. Until for this short duration it has been possible to stand facing the dog with the lead slack, no attempt should be made to make any other movement. The progression is to stand one pace away from the dogs nose, still using the lead held above his neck should it be necessary to hold him steady. Once this is successfully accomplished, then assuming that the dog sits in the middle of a clock facing the handler who is at 6 o'clock, several positions should be adopted round the dog by moving between 3 and 9 o'clock round the bottom part of the dial. Until perfectly steady when standing in front and to the side of him, do not attempt to adopt positions to his rear. Remember that it will be the dogs natural reaction at first to follow your movements with his head, which if you are behind him, he will have difficulty in doing without moving his feet. At all times whilst the lead is kept slack above the dogs head, care must be taken not to suddenly tighten it, for this will be likely to precipitate movement. However if he does attempt to move then the lead must again be held tight above his head to keep him still.

A lead connected to the collar but not held by the trainer still retains a certain amount of restraining influence over a dog. As a transition from using the lead to lead free training, lay it out on the ground in front of him then starting with the first movement described at the beginning of this chapter proceed through the same sequence. If he attempts to move pick up the lead continuing the training with it held in the hand, but whilst he remains steady give occasional reassuring praise. Before attempting to practise stays without the lead attached certain basic princliples must be established. If the dog attempts to move, rather than repeat the command from a distance, return to his side to make him steady in the original place, then give the command and signal before moving away again. If he moves repeatedly he is not yet ready to be left without the restricting influence of the lead, or premature attempts are being made to put too great a distance between dog and handler. The answer is the same as nearly all training exercises and that is to revert to the previously successful stage for further practise. Whilst giving a second or subsequent commands from a distance might appear to the handler to have the desired effect, it can in fact have the opposite effect. The dog may think that he can move when he wishes because if he is wrong he will be told, so why bother to stop still when the trainers reaction can be tested at any time.

Great care must be taken with the hands, for dogs learn to watch their movements although we may not be aware of it. Tit-bits and most training involves the hands so it becomes natural for the dog to observe every movement they make. In fact the more highly trained a dog becomes the greater is the care that should be taken with the hands. A dog that is being trained to come when called by an oral command plus hand signals towards the body, can hardly be blamed for moving from a stay if the handler unconsciously makes recall hand movements. It may sound quite logical when explained in this manner, but it is surprising how many people do not realise the confusion that is caused by not thinking of these things.

Another principle of stay training is to be in a position to immediately return to the dog should he move, rather than relax for a cup of tea or a chat to a friend only to realise that he may have moved some time ago. This is one of the most difficult parts of stay training for we have already established that correction or reward must be instantaneous with the dogs actions. With the handler more than a few feet away from the dog it becomes impossible to take instant measures to put him right.

When training this exercise there is no such thing as correction in the strict sense of the word. Success is achieved by always returning to the dog should he move to put him back in the original position prior to leaving him again. This is another example of the benefits to be gained from attendance at a dog training club. Not only will it be possible for the instructor to put your dog back in place, but distractions will happen that cannot be simulated in the quiet of the home, and will help to make the dog steady under many conditions. A further advantage is that usually all the dogs in the class practise stay training at the same time, thus each dog has to learn to ignore the temptation to go to a fellow canine. All these points are of advantage if it is the desire to own a well trained dog who will remain so under almost any circumstances.

Having established these princliples of training a stay without the lead attached, commence practise following the same positional clock sequence as described earlier. Once the dog is perfectly steady then the time has come to move progressively further away from him, perhaps adding two paces distance over a period of time until he can be safely left by 10 to 12 paces for approximately two minutes.

Until he is capable of remaining stationary when the handler stands apparently disinterested with his back to the dog, no attempt must be made to move out of sight. When doing so it must only be for a few seconds at first, for remember the aim is to build confidence rather than to see how long he will stay without moving.

If the dog barks when left in a stay ignore him at first, but should it continue do not return to correct him, for he will be achieving his object of calling you back. In this case use a friend or someone the dog trusts as the person who will go to him for the purpose of chastising him without inciting movement.

The down stay is practised in exactly the same way

as the 'Sit Stay', although practising one position directly following another is risking problems. If this is done frequently the dog may start anticipating the next exercise, going from the sit to the down or vice versa.

Tit-bits are very useful as rewards for a job well done, but it is not wise to use them during stay training for fear that as the handler returns he will move in his eagerness to get them. More suitable is to return to his side for a few seconds before walking once round him, then giving lavish praise.

*The stay well trained*

## Reminders

1. Do not use the word 'Stay' if practising a recall.

2. Give a flat left hand signal in conjunction with the command.

3. Repeat the command and tighten the lead each time the dog attempts to move.

4. When the lead is slackened without the dog moving, praise him.

5. Don't over-praise the dog or he will be encouraged to move.

6. Only leave him for a few seconds at first.

7. Be careful not to wave the hands around.

8. If the dog moves return to him, never give further commands from a distance.

9. Make haste slowly.

# Chapter 8

# COME WHEN CALLED

## The Recall

This subject has been deliberately left to the latter part of the book as other chapters have explained some elementary recall principles. It is certainly not because the recall is unimportant, far from it, for a dog that will not come when he is called is not worth owning. There has to be mutual love and respect rather than a one sided affair of the dog "cocking a snoot" when he is called. As such he is not "man's best friend" but an animal whose only regard for his human friends is when he wants attention or food. Therefore an immediate response to his name and the recall command is the most basic part of dog ownership which must be conquered above all else.

In the chapter entitled "Educating the Puppy" we explained how simple it is to teach a puppy to respond to his name and the command, but many people do not realise they have a problem until the puppy has become an adult. There are also people who for various reasons take on an adult dog that has had little or no training, who only returns to the handler in his own good time. This chapter is designed to help such people and to continue the education of a puppy that has been channelled in the right direction.

Just as a puppy can have early recall lessons without being taught to sit still first, so can the adult dog. With the handle of the lead held in the right hand walk forward with the dog on your left side. Immediately both dog and handler are going forward, or if he instantly pulls to the end of the lead, suddenly start walking slowly backwards while calling his name followed by the command 'Come'. As he responds tell him he is a 'Good Boy' and when he arrives halt, using the three aids to place him into a straight sit. Remember that the right arm holds the lead reasonably tight above the dogs head, the command 'Sit' is given while placing him with the aid of the left hand into a straight sit in what is known as "the present position". All this must be done simultaneously, firmly and gently, with praise immediately following the required response. If a tit-bit has been secreted in one hand, this can be given to him once he is steady, followed by more praise before moving away to indicate that it is all over for the moment. This training sequence can be repeated several times in one session, but remember to play with the dog now and again between attempts. It cannot be overstressed that the dog must regard recall training as great fun, always wishing to return to the handler as quickly as possible because it is such a pleasurable experience. If that interesting sound was used with the young puppy there is no reason why it cannot still be included to ensure a speedy return.

Once the dog will sit still the time has come to advance the training a little by leaving him in the sit which will be reasonably simple if he has been taught to stay, and if not just a little patience is required. First of all we must establish again the golden rule that there must be no confusion between the command 'Stay' *(I will return to you)* and 'Wait' *(I shall eventually call you).* At no time should the command 'Stay' be used if the dog is to be called from where he has been left, for it will only encourage him to move from a stay at a later date.

Place the dog in the sit at heel position holding the lead in the right hand but letting it run over the left hand slightly above the dogs head so that it is taut. Once sure that the dog is steady give the command 'Wait', then using the right leg, step slightly to his side before moving round to face him. This step to the side with the right foot is to avoid any confusion with heelwork where the exercise commences by moving the left foot directly forward. After a few attempts the dog should begin to understand what is required, therefore making it possible to relax the tension on the lead while keeping the hand above his head so that sufficient tension can be applied to the lead again if necessary. After having remained in front of the dog for a few seconds, return to his side, remembering that sitting still while the handler moves takes the dog a little while to learn. Once he has got the idea and the lead can be totally relaxed, take two or three backward paces away from him, returning to stand straight in front of his nose after a short interval. Finally walk round the dog to the heel position keeping the lead taut above his head while doing so. Without requiring the dog to move he can be praised after each stage, although he has hopefully done nothing other than learn the correct heel and present position by remaining stationary. Of course it will take time for the message to sink in, so do not go through the routine just the once but rather several times over many sessions.

Once these movements have been perfected the training can become a little more advanced. Place the dog at heel in the sit position holding the handle of the lead in the right hand. Give the command 'Wait' then walk to the end of the lead by first taking a small pace to the right with the right foot. It is essential that whilst carrying out this manoeuvre the lead remains slack, for the slightest tightening of it will encourage him to anticipate what follows. With a dog that is still not entirely trustworthy to the command 'Wait' it may be found easier to walk backwards to the end of the lead, thus being in a position to watch his movements the whole time. Once in position do not immediately call the dog, or after very few attempts at this exercise he will associate the act of turning to face him with being called. Having waited a few seconds give the command 'Fido Come' at the same time flicking both hands to the groin which will have the effect of bringing the dog forward, and as he comes gather the lead in keeping it very slightly tight. The reader may think that the hands going to the groin is of little importance, but this is a signal which will eventually be remembered by the dog just as much as the command. When the time comes for practising the recall without the lead the dog will associate this hand movement with the previous lead action, making the transition to recalls without the lead that much easier for him to understand. It is important that at all times the command is simultaneous with the hand movement, or apprehension may be the result with the dog hesitating before coming.

Once the dog has arrived almost in front of you, if necessary take one or two paces backwards until his backbone is straight with your body before giving the command 'Sit'. If he is slow to sit in the present position, lean quickly forward to tap his backside whilst repeating the command. However a timely word of warning is rather than do this too often, practise quick obedience to the sit command in the heel position. Leaning over the dog is always to be

WAIT
WAIT
FIDO
COME

*Recall lessons*

avoided as much as possible, for this together with the tap on his backside may well make him sit further away next time. Therefore rather than curing a fault the handler has created another, as faults are rarely the dogs mistake but rather those caused by the one who seeks to train him. The same thing applies to the dog that is slow to come, for in such cases it is usually because he has become apprehensive for reasons of the handlers errors. Some of these may be bad timing of the lead flick and command, too heavy a jerk on the lead, the training aids used in the wrong order, or too harsh a tone of voice. Always remember that the recall command is a request to be used in a happy tone conveying an association of pleasure to the dog. Never pull the dog towards you with the lead, and during recall training never take any action that he will find distasteful.

If the handler wishes to teach the dog to sit straight there are several aids that can be used, but it is not an easy thing to achieve. Dependent on the size of the dog, always stand with the feet slightly apart so that there is room for his paws just inside the tip of the shoes. Avoid standing with the feet at angles, keeping them parallel instead. Twisting the body may straighten the dog, but it will not teach him to sit straight when such a signal is not given. Grabbing the dog to pull him in only achieves the opposite of the desired effect, for the fact that it is necessary is caused by apprehension or a lack of understanding and will only make matters worse. The best way is to stand upright throughout the exercise, flicking the hands to the groin when giving the command, and as the dog approaches leaning slightly back while drawing the hands up to the chest. It is more than likely that the dog will watch the hands, particularly if they have held a tit-bit in the past, and the fact that he will have to look up to watch them will help to straighten him prior to sitting, so never keep them too low or wave them about.

In order to repeat this exercise do not attempt to send the dog to heel (the finish) but, having praised him for a job well done, tell him to 'Wait' then walk round him to the heel position. Until the dog has perfected recall training, persistent practise of the finish following the recall will only encourage him to sit crooked in anticipation of the next direction in which he will be required to go.

As a transition to recall training without the lead, go through the usual sequence but as he comes run backwards a few steps, gradually gathering in the lead prior to bringing the hands to the chest and halting. A crafty dog may think that once the lead is not attached he can do as he pleases, so first practise

*Dispensing with the lead*

several recalls on the lead. With the dog ready in the heel position, quietly unclip the lead but use it in exactly the same manner so that he thinks he is still under its controlling influence.

Over a period of time increase the distance between you and the dog without ever trying to run before you can walk. Whilst remembering that the greater the distance between handler and dog will mean the faster he returns, make haste slowly always reverting to the previous stage if he fails to succeed with more advanced training.

Both over enthusiastic and nervous dogs are prone to anticipate the recall by moving before the handler gives the command. If this is the case do not worry, for if the dog has to have faults then anticipation is a good one. Attendance at a dog training club will enable you to be shown how to cure the problem, for the dog will very often be expected to remain steady in a line of fellow canines prior to being called. Whilst you may think this would aggravate the problem, the answer is that to ensure a dog will remain steady under almost any circumstances, this provocation of stopping still while other dogs are called is necessary. If he moves while other dogs are being called take a pace towards him immediately he attempts to do so, but if he is already on his way just call him rather than attempting to push him back into position for this action may well subdue a speedy return. In future return to stand in front of him without making any attempt to call him, for by doing so you will be teaching the meaning of the command 'Wait' which is really all that is wrong. The same cure applies to the dog that will not let the handler get away at all before moving. It is only a case of forgetting the recall and training the dog to wait. With such a dog go back to the original training sequence but rather than call him, walk once round him before giving praise for being so clever. This will probably be necessary over quite a period of time even to the extent of not calling the dog on three occasions out of four although it may appear that he has learned.

## The Recall to Heel

When walking in the country and it becomes expedient for the dog to come to heel without the handler stopping, another type of recall is the answer. This is generally referred to in dog training clubs as the Class 'A' recall simply because it is a test used in that type of competition. If belonging to a club do not expect to be taught this movement until the dog has become proficient at all other exercises, for it is a little advanced. However for those who

*The recall to heel*

wish to train on their own the following is the way to proceed. With the dog sitting in the heel position attach the lead to his training collar then hold the handle in the left hand. Tell the dog 'Wait' before stepping off by moving the right leg first so that there is no confusion with heelwork training. As the end of the lead is reached call 'Fido Heel' simultaneously flicking the lead whilst continuing to walk encouraging the dog to join you at heel. As he arrives remember to praise him then start again. After several training sessions the dog will start to beat the flick of the lead acting just on the command, this will be an indication to the handler to attempt the exercise lead free. So start just a few paces away from him and increase the distance as he learns. A timely word of warning is that unless the dog is proficient at walking to heel without the lead, then to attempt teaching this kind of recall is courting disaster. No doubt the reader has noticed that the command is 'Heel' and not 'Come', so it follows that the dog must already understand and obey this command. As in all training if progress is being made too quickly for the dog, revert to the previously successful stage until he has learned.

### The Finish

Sending the dog from the present to the heel position is known as 'the finish'. It is not an essential training exercise for a domestic pet, but nevertheless is a useful way of returning the dog to heel after calling him into the present. If envisaging any competition work this exercise is essential, but most dog training clubs show pet owners how to teach the finish to give the handler greater control even though competition is not their aim.

To avoid any likelihood of the dog anticipating

the exercise or sitting crooked in the direction in which he will be required to go after the present, it is essential that at first the finish is treated as a separate exercise to the recall. Therefore always commence practise by telling the dog to sit before standing in front of him rather than calling him in.

Holding the lead in the left hand loop it behind the right knee, then taking a step back with the right leg, give the command 'Heel'. This will have two effects, the back of the right leg will tighten the lead taking the dog in the required direction, while the fact that the leg is no longer in the way will encourage him to move past the right side of the handler. As the dog reaches the right leg it is replaced to its original position thus leaving him room to go round the back of the legs, whilst by controlling the lead in the left hand and using vocal encouragement he will be drawn into the heel position. As soon as he arrives change the lead to the right hand so that "the three aids" can be used to ensure a quick, close, straight sit, then praise him.

If at first the dog is reluctant to go round the back of the legs to the heel position do not worry. Should this be the case take several steps forward calling his name and the command 'Heel' while tapping the right leg to indicate the correct position. Soon it will become necessary to move forward for the dog will quickly learn what is required.

Once the dog is becoming proficient the training can be advanced. Standing in front of the dog in the present position with the lead held in the left hand, allow it to loop almost to the ground. Having started the dog moving by giving the command 'Heel' the lead will follow him round your legs enabling the amount of slack to be adjusted, so that when he reaches the heel position he can only sit close. Whilst initially it may be necessary to continue taking a step

*Teaching the finish*

back with the right foot, this movement can soon be left out. The three aids must still be used for the sit if you wish the dog to become reliable. Once the dog is executing a perfect finish on the lead an attempt can be made to practise the exercise lead free. If his execution is still perfect then all is well, if not revert to lead training until he understands all the component parts of the finish.

There is another way that the dog can be taught to finish and that is by moving straight round to the left rather than going behind the handlers legs. This is a little more difficult to teach but if you think it is desirous, your local dog training club will advise.

# Chapter 9

# OTHER LIKELY PROBLEMS

## How to Tie a Dog Securely and Safely

If asked how to tie a dog many peoples reactions would be "why do I need to learn to tie a knot?". With a little thought it becomes apparent that it is not quite as simple as this. If the dog is tied 8 or 10 inches from the ground and subsequently gets up to move, the lead can wrap round his legs several times causing distress or injury. Always tie a dog up rather than down, door knob height is appropriate, which will not allow the dog to become entangled with the lead. Door knobs themselves are not suitable places to tie a dog for someone may unwittingly injure him while opening or closing the door.

When tieing a dog never use a piece of string or anything that a young puppy or dog can easily chew through. If he is a chewer then that expensive training lead will quickly be in two pieces, so use a chain which will render him secure.

Never tie dogs to objects that are not absolutely secure in themselves. Tieing to a pram is particularly dangerous if there is a baby inside, just as tieing to bicycles or chairs is hazardous. A dog that has been frightened will take off with any movable object being towed behind, causing him much stress and even greater fear.

## Over Protective Dogs

People are often heard to say how well the dog protects their wife or child, which is desirous to a certain extent. However, the owner must take care that the dog does not become over-protective to any member of the family, particularly children Situations can arise where the over-protective dog, not understanding that a mock fight is really play, will bite the one he considers to be attacking. Parties are a good example, for often the children are screaming in fun or running around, thus stimulating the dogs protective tendencies. This type of dog must either be confined to a room where he will be safe or tied up away from the children.

Some dogs when tied will protect their immediate surrounds although they would not do so if not secured by the lead. A dog such as this, although secured by the lead must never be left in a public place for someone may attempt to stroke him only to be bitten as they approach. Such action is also caused by the dog feeling restricted by the lead and unable to protect himself properly. He therefore assumes everyone to be a danger to him, adopting the adage of "attack being the best method of defence"

No matter what breed or of what size, an over-protective dog or one with any aggressive tendencies must always be put in a safe place when in public and when strangers enter the house

## Reactions to Telephones and Door Bells

It is somewhat disconcerting to own a dog that goes berserk when the telephone or door bell rings. Invariably this has been caused by members of the household stimulating excitement in the dog by rushing to answer them. If you own such a dog or wish to avoid this association of ideas, analyse the family's reactions to door and telephone bells then issue strict instructions that in future such calls must be answered in a calm and reasonably leisurely manner. Of course the dog that has already developed such a bad habit will need to be taught that his behaviour is anti-social. To do so enlist the help of a friend to ring the door bell or make a call by telephone. Prior to the pre-arranged time tie the dog securely to his place in the house and at the first sign of excitement, immediately calm him or if necessary severely vocally chastise him. As soon as he reacts favourably, gently praise the dog to indicate that his lack of reaction is correct. A bad case will not be cured in one evening, so dependent upon the success achieved it will be necessary for several calls to be made in any session and for the sessions to be continued until the dog has learned to remain calm. Once taught how to behave when bells ring, the family must continue to make a leisurely response to them. After all, if the call is of any importance the caller will allow sufficient time for someone to answer or try again later.

In extreme cases of such behaviour it has been known for members of the household to be bitten during the dogs excitement, so if possible never allow the dog to develop such neurosis, or take immediate steps to correct it.

### Asking for Food at the Table

A dog that is allowed to sit beside the dining table during meal times will very soon develop the habit of asking for food. This can happen in various ways, he may bark, whine, nudge with his paws or nose, or just sit there dribbling from the mouth while his eyes appeal for a tit-bit. Such behaviour has been taught to the dog by allowing him near the table looking sorry for himself to provoke sympathy. This behaviour may be acceptable amongst the members of the household but it can become an embarrassment when guests are present, particularly if they are not exactly dog lovers.

The prevention or cure is never to allow the dog in the vicinity of a meal table, if necessary tieing him to his place in the house where he will be unable to see food being eaten and thus incited to beg for it.

## Dogs and Rubbish Bins

Dogs can become artful, quickly learning how to open the kitchen waste bin. Not only is it unhygienic and annoying to find kitchen waste spread over the floor, but the bin might contain refuse such as chicken bones which can be harmful to the dog should he consume them. The best answer to this problem is prevention rather than cure, by keeping the bin out of the dogs reach or by placing a weight on it. Alternatively the dog must never be allowed in the kitchen unattended, thus making such action impossible.

The same problem and likely preventions apply to the dust bin which should be constructed in such a way that the lid can be secured. An alternative, if there is room to do so, might be to build a brick compound to house the bin.

If the dog is caught in the act then some remonstration with him will help, but unless able to do this on every occasion, he will not be completely reliable when left on his own.

## Dogs on Furniture

The average housewife doesn't want her home turned into a kennel, therefore it is wise to only allow the dog in certain rooms, teaching him never to cross pre-determined thresholds. Neither is it good practise to allow dogs on to chairs or beds, with the result that people subsequently using them find hairs adhered to their clothing. Even more annoying is for a small piece of biscuit to drop down the back of a chair that the dog may be on, for it has been known for dogs to tear a chair to pieces to get to the biscuit.

A dog having a place of his own with a bed raised slightly from the floor to avoid ground draughts, should never need to climb on to furniture. When not in his bed his place is on the floor, so when the dog makes any attempt to get up on to a chair he must be reprimanded and given the command 'Off' Soon he will come to learn the meaning of this word, but do beware of saying 'Down' for such a command is to be reserved to teach the dog to lie down when told. If the word has two meanings the dog can only become confused. Do not make the mistake of thinking that it is alright when he is a puppy for he will not understand why he shouldn't do so when he becomes older. What a dog has never had he never misses, so be kind to him by making the rules clear from the beginning.

A possible problem often overlooked by owners of small breeds that are allowed on to furniture is that an older person is not always aware of something being on a chair. If they inadvertently sit on the dog the shock of the sudden squealing can cause a heart attack. Small breeds can be hidden by a cushion so it is not always the more elderly that will not see them, but if the dog is taught not to climb on to furniture this problem can be avoided.

## Jumping up at People

Dogs that jump up to greet people can be a nuisance even though it may be acceptable to the owner. Muddy paws on clothing is an obvious possible result, but sometimes the dogs claws can damage clothing. As with nearly all training problems they are caused by the owners who, in this case, allow the small puppy to jump up making a fuss of him whilst he does so. Right from the first day the puppy comes home he should be ignored when he jumps up and only fondled when he has four feet on the ground. It is far better to go down to him for fuss and reassurance than to let him to jump up. It may appear cute to allow the small puppy to do this, but if a large breed is encouraged to do so when young, as an adult dog why should he suddenly understand that knocking people over, planting his paws on their chests or shoulders is unacceptable. It is really another case of starting off as you intend to go on. Unfortunately it may be that the owner did not realise the problem being created when the puppy was young, so that some form of action to train an adult dog has become necessary. One way is to tell the dog to sit just before he reaches you, and until he has done so he should not be given any affection. If this is not effective then other cures may be necessary. One such way is to tie the dog on the end of a four foot lead, then approaching him on numerous occasions, stop just short of him so that when he attempts to jump up the lead checks him whilst you simultaneously use the command 'Off'. Another alternative is to allow someone else to handle the dog so that you can approach him giving the command 'Off' whilst the assistant checks the dog in mid-flight.

There is a more severe way of curing the problem which should only be used when all else fails. As the dog jumps give the command and raise the knee sideways to give him a little bump in the chest that will knock him off. It is useless to push the dog down with the hands as he will keep jumping towards them, considering it to be a good game. Usually the more this is done the worse the problem becomes.

### Opening Doors and Switching on Lights

Some dogs become very artful, quickly learning how to open doors that have a handle with a down movement by putting their paws on them. The only satisfactory way to stop this is to change such handles for the turning knob type. If this means replacing all the household door handles it can become expensive, so therefore an alternative may be to reverse the handle so that the door is opened when the handle is turned upwards.

The same answer applies to the dog that switches on lights. The switch is best turned upside down. This problem is caused by the dog watching the hand movement on the switch when you enter and leave a room, jumping up to sniff where the hand has been thus inadvertently turning on the light as he does so. It is rarely a case of the dog being very clever wishing to have the light on, but just an automatic reaction to detect his owners scent on the place that he last saw the hand.

### Dogs on Stairs and Escalators

Some dogs get the habit of lying on stairways which can be very dangerous. One of the authors kept Whippets many years ago, one of which always preferred to sleep on the broad step at the bend of the stairway. As in farce it occurred to him that a good way to get rid of a mother-in-law would be to give her breakfast in bed, then when she took the tray down stairs, expect to find her at the bottom of the stairs with a broken neck! This is of course a light hearted aside, but it illustrates well the danger of allowing a dog to sleep in such a place.

Many people live in bungalows and when taking the dog on public transport find it necessary to use a staircase. If not previously taught how to negotiate stairs, a dog can become panic stricken when faced with them. One of the authors has owned a dog who would splay his four legs making them rigid rather than be forced to go up or down stairs, and when he did move he would rush at six at a time. Many months of patient teaching became necessary to overcome his fears.

Before risking missing a train because the dog will not use the stairs, try him on a staircase with time to gently teach him how to tackle them one at a time.

Open plan staircases present problems for dogs that are quite happy on solid ones. In this case the fact that they can see through them tends to cause a fear of the stairs being unstable. If it is really necessary to use such stairways then the only answer will be to spend time teaching the dog just two or three steps at a time, using tit-bits if necessary. Do not make the mistake of putting the dog at the top of the stairs to see if he will walk down, for it will be more likely that he will attempt to jump, land half way, falling to the bottom and breaking his neck in the process.

Dogs have a fear of anything that appears unstable, and escalators are no exception. Getting the dog on to one is difficult enough, but trying to encourage him to disembark is almost an impossibility. Unless prepared to carry the dog never take him anywhere if using an escalator will be unavoidable.

## Sea and Air Travel

Nowadays people are much more widely travelled than of old, so the possibility of taking the dog somewhere by sea or air may arise. If it is to be outside of the country of domicile, the first thing to do is to understand the quarantine laws of the two countries involved. This seems obvious advice but what many people overlook are the regulations of the carrier. For example you may wish a dog to travel by sea or air within the confines of the United Kingdom quarantine laws, it being quite acceptable to take a dog to the Channel Isles. If he is to travel by air then the airline will insist that he travels in a special crate in the freight compartment. If travelling by British Rail Sealink he can either remain in the car for the duration of the journey or he must be crated on deck.

If there is advanced warning of a trip where crating will be necessary, then it is much kinder to the dog to accustom him to the crate prior to the journey. To do so, ascertain the type of crate to be used ensuring that it has sufficient ventilation, then make up a mock one and start getting him used to stopping in it. First he can be fed in it on two or three occasions, then starting with short intervals leave him in the crate, building up the duration of time to coincide with that of the journey to be undertaken. In such a way it may be possible to save the dog unnecessary fretting.

Remember that should you take the dog by air on a United Kingdom domestic flight and for any reason the plane is forced to divert to another country, then on return to the United Kingdom the dog will be required to undergo six months quarantine.

## General Advice

There are many other training problems that a dog owner may have to contend with. To specify and suggest a cure to all that have come to our notice over the years would require a book on this subject alone. If your particular training problem is not mentioned within these pages, read the chapter entitled "Dog Training Principles", then establish the true cause of the dogs behaviour before attempting a possible cure.

Training dogs is all about common sense, logic, being firm, consistency of action, timing and kindness and we hope we have made this clear. If by reading this book your dog becomes a credit to you, we will have achieved our object.

# INDEX

# DOG TRAINING CLUBS

*Dog Training Clubs are listed alphabetically under counties, showing the name of the club, the training day, which in most cases are evenings, the nearest town to the venue and the secretary's name and telephone number.*

*If there is no dog training club listed for your area The Kennel Club, 1-4 Clarges Street, Piccadilly, London W1Y 8AB will be able to advise the location of the nearest club to your address.*

### BEDFORDSHIRE

DUNSTABLE & DISTRICT DOG TRAINING CLUB Monday/Wednesday, Dunstable. Mrs. M. Richardson.

### BERKSHIRE

NEWBURY & DISTRICT DOG TRAINING SOCIETY Friday, Newbury. Mrs. S. White, Thatcham 67217

### CAMBRIDGESHIRE

ST.IVES (HUNTINGDON) DOG TRAINING CLUB Monday, Fenstanton. Mrs. G. Baxter, St. Ives 63427.

WHITTLESEY DOG TRAINING SOCIETY Monday/Tuesday, Peterborough. Mrs. S. Rhodes, Peterborough 241501

### CHESHIRE

DANESFORD OBEDIENCE DOG TRAINING CLUB Tuesday/Thursday, Congleton. Mrs. J. Blythe, Congleton 71486.

### CLEVELAND

MIDDLESBROUGH & DISTRICT DOG TRAINING ASSOC Monday/Thursday, Middlesbrough. Mrs. J. Nesbitt Stockton 586474

### CORNWALL

FALMOUTH & DICTRICT DOG TRAINING CLUB Wednesday Falmouth. Miss L.C. Peploe, St. Day 820364

### CUMBRIA

BORDER DOG TRAINING CLUB Wednesday Carlisle Mrs. M. Clegg, Carlisle 21644.

### DUNBARTON

LENNOX DOG TRAINING CLUB Thursday Dunbarton Miss Netta Plenderleith, Dunbarton 64750

## ESSEX

VANGE & DISTRICT DOG TRAINING CLUB Monday, Basildon. Mr. J. F. Field, Basildon 20769.

CLACTON & DISTRICT DOG TRAINING CLUB Monday, Clacton. Mrs. Halina Kochanowski, St. Osyth 820444.

GREAT DUNMOW & DISTRICT DOG CLUB Monday, Great Dunmow, Mrd. A. Monk, Great Dunmow 3265.

## GLOUCESTERSHIRE

TEWKESBURY & DISTRICT DOG TRAINING CLUB Tuesday, Tewkesbury. Miss S.M. Millichap, Bredon 72666.

## GWENT

CWMBRAN & DISTRICT DOG TRAINING CLUB Monday, Pontypool. Mr. K.W.G. Hunt, Usk 2975.

## HAMPSHIRE

ALTON & DISTRICT DOG TRAINING SOCIETY Tuesday, Alton. Mr. W. F. Oliver, Alton 63634.

GOSPORT & DISTRICT DOG TRAINING CLUB Wednesday, Gosport. Mr. D. J. Fleming, Horndean 592927.

HASLEMERE & DISTRICT DOG TRAINING CLUB – Thursday, Grayshott. Mrs. C.C. Guard, Liphook 722779.

LYMINGTON & DISTRICT DOG TRAINING CLUB – Thursday, Hordle. Mrs. B. Dunford, New Milton 616666.

PORTSMOUTH & DISTRICT DOG TRAINING CLUB – Thursday, Portsmouth. Mrs. N. Robbins, Portsmouth 24372.

SOLENT DOG TRAINING SOCIETY Monday, Waterlooville Mr. F.C. Wright, Emsworth 5318.

## HERTFORDSHIRE

NORTH HERTS DOG TRAINING CLUB Tuesday/Friday, Hitchin. Mrs. E.K. Hood, Stevenage 55771.

RADLETT DOG TRAINING SOCIETY Friday, Radlett. Mr. J. Saner, Radlett 6268.

HERTFORD & DISTRICT DOG TRAINING SOCIETY Thursday, Ware. Mrs. J. Kebble, Royston 72794.

## ISLE OF MAN

ISLE OF MAN DOG OBEDIENCE CLUB Tuesday, Douglas. Mr. Eric Quirk, 0624-82-2572.

## KENT

ASHFORD (KENT) DOG TRAINING CLUB Thursday, Ashford. Miss Barbara Butcher, Ashford 20954.

SEVENOAKS & DISTRICT DOG TRAINING SOCIETY Monday & Thursday, Sevenoaks. Mrs. Y.V.B. Turner, Knockholt 2116.

SHEPWAY DOG TRAINING CLUB Monday, Folkestone
Mrs. J.C. Moate, Kearsney 3152.

TANKERTON & NORTH EAST KENT DOG TRAINING CLUB
Tuesday, Whitstable. Mr. J.E. Gascoigne, Whitstable 262903.

TANKERTON & NORTH EAST KENT DOG TRAINING CLUB
Wednesday/Thursday, Herne Bay. Mr. J.E. Gascoigne, Whitstable 262903.

## LANCASHIRE

MID LANCS DOG TRAINING CLUB Wednesday, Rochdale.
Miss Angela L. Howarth, Rochdale 58870.

## LEICESTERSHIRE

MELTON MOWBRAY DOG TRAINING CLUB – Thursday, Melton Mowbray. Mrs. M. Jackson, Melton Mowbray 4786.

## LONDON

BECKENHAM DOG TRAINING CLUB Thursday, Beckenham.
Mrs. G.C. Davie, 01-656-9975.

FRIERN DOG TRAINING CLUB - Wednesday, North London.
Miss P.M. Pryke, 01-445-2148.

MOORE PARK DOG TRAINING CLUB - Wednesday, London.
Mrs. A. McHarg, 01-381-2851.

## MERSEYSIDE

SOUTHPORT ALSATIAN TRAINING CLUB Thursday
Southport. Mrs. Val Carr, Southport 31276. (Mrs. James).

## MIDDLESEX

ENFIELD CHACE DOG TRAINING CLUB Wednesday, Enfield
Mr C.M. Plum, 01-360-6298.

## NORTHAMPTONSHIRE

RUSHDEN AND DISTRICT DOG TRAINING CLUB Friday
Rushden. Mr T.P Benjamin, Rushden 56728.

## NORTH YORKSHIRE

RIPON DOG TRAINING SOCIETY Monday Ripon
Mrs. M. Glover, Ripon 2941

## OXFORDSHIRE

KIDLINGTON ALL BREEDS DOG TRAINING SOCIETY
Tuesday, Oxford. Miss P.M. Belcher, Cumnor 2550

KIDLINGTON ALL BREEDS DOG TRAINING SOCIETY
Wednesday, Oxford. Mrs. N Scott, Oxford 881214 (Ringcraft)

## RENFREWSHIRE

GLENIFFER DOG TRAINING CLUB Monday, Barrhead. Mrs. J.T. McIlroy, 041-881-5672.

## SOMERSET

MENDIP & DISTRICT DOG TRAINING SOCIETY Thursday, Wells. Mrs. Janet Goodwin, Street 45069.

## SUFFOLK

GIPPING & DISTRICT DOG TRAINING CLUB Monday & Wednesday, Ipswich. Mr. S.E. Taylor, Ipswich 830636.

## SURREY

BAGSHOT CANINE TRAINING SCHOOL – Tuesday, Bagshot. Mrs. M. Smith, Chobham 8562.

CLANDON DOG TRAINING SOCIETY Monday, Guildford. Mrs. J. Nicholl, Woking 63421.

NEWLANDS WORKING DOG SOCIETY Thursday, Guildford. Mrs. V.H. Upton, Shere 2006.

SURREY DOG TRAINING SOCIETY Monday, Guildford. Miss J. Smith, Brookwood 5503.

SURREY DOG TRAINING SOCIETY Tuesday, Knaphill. Miss J. Smith, Brookwood 5503.

## SUSSEX

DENNE PARK DOG TRAINING CLUB Wednesday & Thursday, Horsham. Mrs. V. Stone, Horsham 4614.

DOG OBEDIENCE GROUP Friday, Hove. Mrs. D. Gearing, Brighton 732896.

HASTINGS & ST.LEONARDS DOG TRAINING CLUB Monday, Hastings. Mrs. Carol Ashby, Bexhill 210656.

WORTHING & LANCING DOG TRAINING CLUB Wednesday & Thursday, Worthing. Mrs. Norris, Worthing 30416.

## WARWICKSHIRE

STONELEIGH DOG TRAINING CLUB Tuesday, Stoneleigh. Miss B. Witheridge, Warwick 42092.

NUNEATON DOG TRAINING CLUB Sunday & Wednesday Nuneaton. Mr. S.J. Courts, 0203-319964.

## WEST MIDLANDS

HAWBUSH DOG TRAINING CLUB Friday, Brierley Hill. Mr. H.C. Price, 0384-67920.

WARLEY & DISTRICT DOG TRAINING CLUB Sunday & Thursday, Oldbury. Mr Harold Bellamy, 021-422-5193.

WIDNEY DOG TRAINING CLUB Sunday or Monday, Solihull Mrs. E.P Chambers, 021 777-3674

YARDLEY & DISTRICT ALSATIAN TRAINING CLUB Sunday, Birmingham. Mrs. Y.D. Morton. Berkswell 33117

## NATIONALLY

**BRITISH ASSOCIATION FOR GERMAN SHEPHERD DOGS — TRAINING ON VARIOUS DAYS OF THE WEEK IN A NUMBER OF TOWNS. For GSD'S (Alsatians) only. Miss M. M. Webb. 021-373-3424.**

DOG TRAINING CLUBS WISHING TO BE INCLUDED IN THIS LIST IN FUTURE EDITIONS PLEASE CONTACT THE PUBLISHERS.

# Your dog's best friend

**Vetzyme**

Phillips Yeast Products., Park Royal Road, London NW10 7JX. Telephone: 01-965 7533.

# ONLY THE BEST IS GOOD ENOUGH FOR TOP DOGS.

Abels veterinary products provide a complete system of dietary supplements to keep top dogs in the peak of condition.

**ABELS' ALL-IN-ONE CONDITIONER** cures all types of worm, eczema and allied skin disorders. 100% safe. Non-poisonous, non-purgative and tasteless. Fully tested by veterinary surgeons who have always supported our claims.

**ABELS' GARLIC TABLETS.** A natural remedy for intestinal infections. For fresh breath too.

**ABELS' CALCIUM WITH VITAMIN D** provides a rich and natural source of calcium to strengthen teeth and bones. (A small amount of Vitamin D in each tablet aids absorption). Important for both puppies and old faithfuls.

**ABELS' VITAMIN E TABLETS** give racing and gundogs the extra energy they need to succeed. Also improves the chances of successful mating by up to 40%. Abels' Vitamin E tablets are reasonably priced too.

**ABELS' ASCORBIC ACID TABLETS.** Vitamin C to maintain tip-top condition in all breeds, and to promote collegen production.

**CURACHO.** A rub for dogs suffering from sprains, bruises or rheumatism. Particularly good for whippets and greyhounds.

**ABELS' SEAWEED TABLETS** for glossy coats and general good health. Also available in powder form or combined with iron in ABELS' SEAWEED AND IRON TABLETS for extra benefit.

**ABEL'S FF GRANS.** Used by breeders to give their pedigree dogs super glossy coats. Don't be too generous with FF Grans if your dog is wire haired!

**ABELS' LIVER TREATS.** The best reward for an obedient dog.

Your dog works hard for you. Make sure he gets the best.

**ABELS' TOP PRODUCTS FOR TOP DOGS**

Send for more details to: **C. F. Abel, Forest Road, Charlbury, Oxfordshire.**

**C. F. ABEL**
**CHARLBURY · OXFORD**